VOLCANOES
Fire and Life

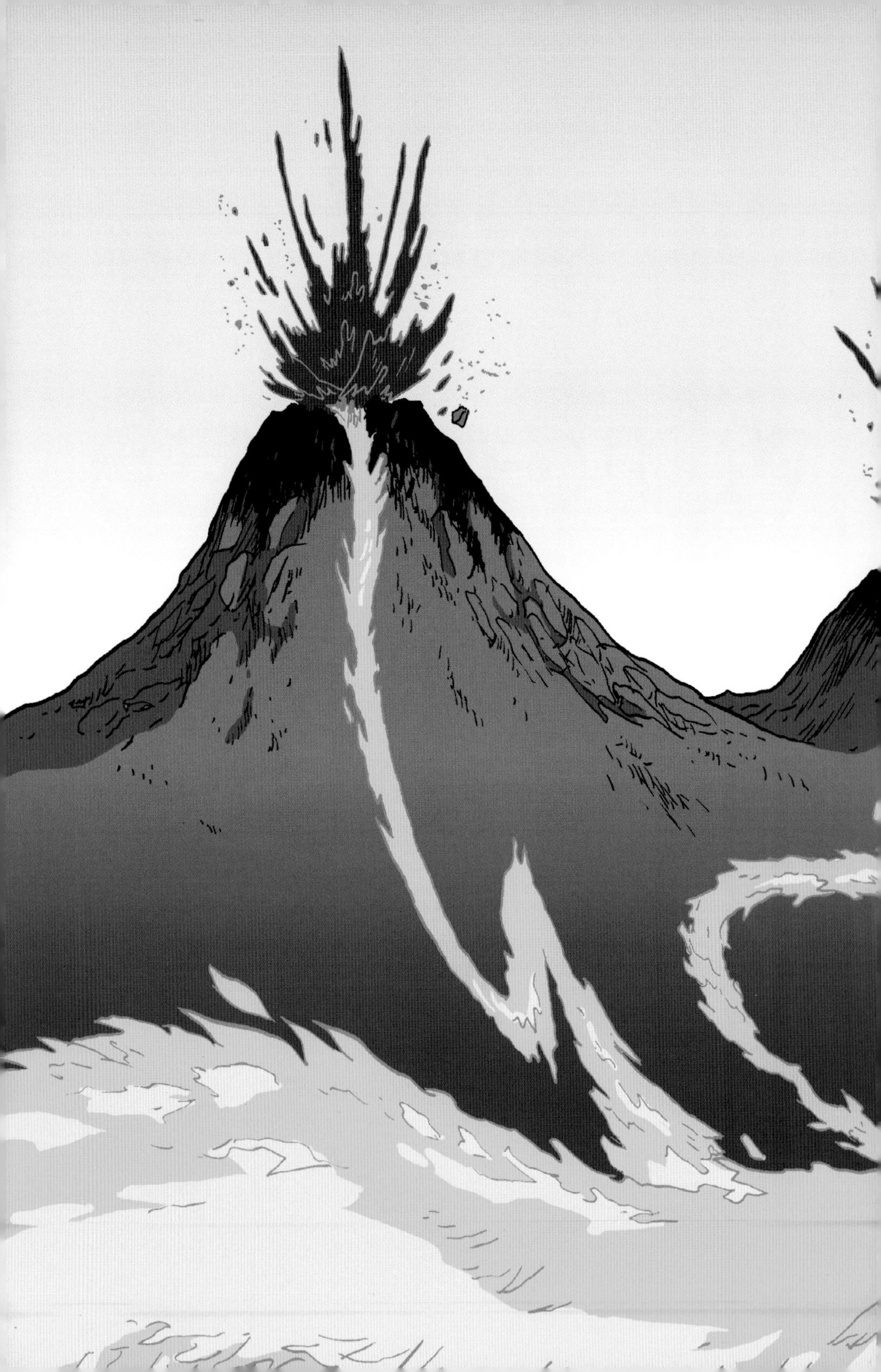

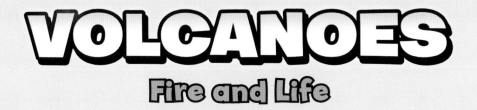

VOLCANOES

Fire and Life

JON CHAD

with color by
Sophie Goldstein

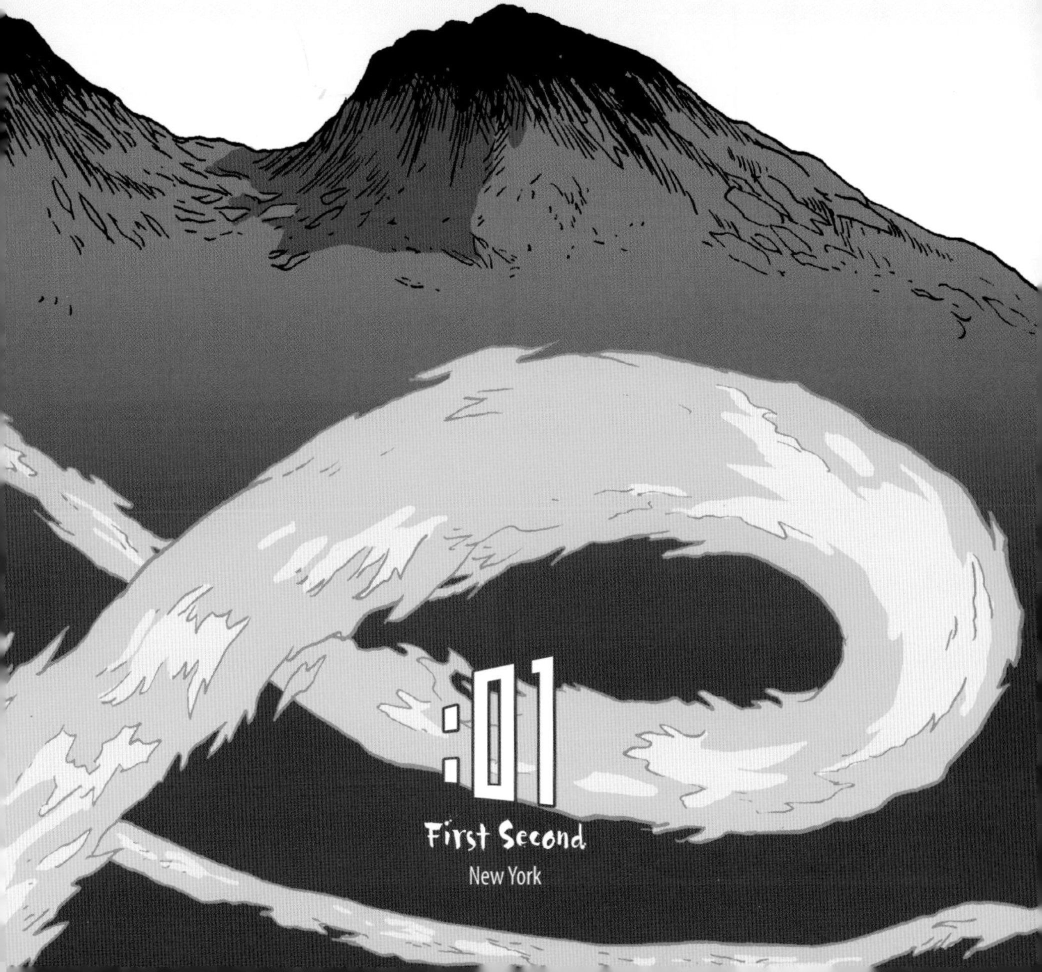

:01
First Second
New York

First Second

Copyright © 2016 by Jon Chad

Drawn on Strathmore 400-series 2-ply smooth bristol board with a Staedtler 4H pencil. The panel borders were drawn with a 1.0 Copic Multiliner and the drawings were inked with a combination of Sakura Micron Pens sizes 08, 05, 03, 02, and 005, and an assortment of drawing nibs including the Hunt 102 Crow Quill, the Hunt 107 Hawk Quill, the Tachikawa No.5 School Pen, and the Tachiwara G-Pen; all dipped in Speedball Superblack ink. Colored using Adobe Photoshop.

Published by First Second
First Second is an imprint of Roaring Brook Press,
a division of Holtzbrinck Publishing Holdings Limited Partnership
120 Broadway, New York, N Y 10271

Cataloging-in-Publication Data is on file at the Library of Congress.

Paperback ISBN 978-1-62672-360-3
Hardcover ISBN 978-1-62672-361-0

Our books may be purchased in bulk for promotional, educational, or business use. Please contact your local bookseller or the Macmillan Corporate and Premium Sales Department at (800) 221-7945 ext. 5442 or by e-mail at MacmillanSpecialMarkets@macmillan.com.

FIRST
EDITION

First edition 2016
Book design by John Green

Printed in China by Toppan Leefung Printing Ltd., Dongguan City, Guandong Province
Paperback: 10
Hardcover: 10 9 8 7 6 5

If you take a hike on a mountain trail, it may feel like the landscape around you has been there forever—mountains look permanent and rivers seem like they have been babbling since the dawn of time. Take a hike with a geologist, however, and you'll hear a different story—one of constant motion and change. We can see our planet's long history in the rocks around us. The rocks tell a story of continents colliding, of Earth's crust ripping, tearing, and grinding, of volcanic explosions and massive earthquakes. The type, size, and shape of rocks can tell us about the slow, gradual changes that create new land and shift continents, and about catastrophic events like asteroid impacts that have altered the entire planet.

Volcanoes are perhaps the most visible and dramatic evidence of these constant changes to the Earth's surface. Volcanic eruptions shape our planet in amazing ways. The very continents we live on have grown and formed because of the movement of magma. Some of Earth's most beautiful natural landmarks like Yosemite National Park, the Rocky Mountains, and Yellowstone National Park are the result of the constant movement of magma from the Earth's interior toward the surface. And let's not forget that many islands, like Hawaii, are the result of volcanic activity on the seafloor!

When you think of volcanoes, you may imagine dangerous eruptions, but volcanic activity benefits us in many ways too. Soil in volcanic regions is often nutrient-rich, making it ideal for growing food. The next time you eat a kiwifruit from New Zealand, keep in mind that the volcanic soil there formed from lava from massive ancient eruptions. Near areas of recent volcanic activity, heat in the crust—known as geothermal energy—can be harnessed to heat homes and generate electricity. Iceland, for instance, is a particularly active volcanic island. And a lot of their electricity and heat is provided free of charge thanks to volcanoes!

As you read, you will learn that each volcano has its own unique personality, just like the characters in this book. When Aurora examines different types of volcanoes—from small flowing eruptions in Hawaii to the massive "super-eruptions" of Yellowstone—she begins to see how different factors like the chemistry of magma and the gasses it contains affect a volcano's eruptions. Aurora takes the time to see beyond volcanoes' intimidating exteriors. She discovers their potential. She learns that volcanoes are sources of land, power, heat, and life! We hope you learn to look at volcanoes a little differently, like Aurora does. Volcanoes may be super hot but the science is super cool!

—Gwyneth Hughes, PhD in Geology, MS Geophysics,
and Michael Cardiff, Assistant Professor in Geoscience, UW–Madison

METRIC MEASUREMENT CONVERSIONS

METRIC		IMPERIAL (US)
1 Millimeter (mm)	≈	0.039 (in)
1 Centimeter (cm)	≈	0.39 (in)
1 Meter (m)	≈	3.28 (ft)
1 Kilometer (km)	≈	0.62 (mi)
1 km per hour	≈	0.62 m per hour
1 Gram (g)	≈	0.002 (lbs)
1 Kilogram (kg)	≈	2.20 (lbs)
1 Liter (l)	≈	0.035 Cubic Feet (ft³)
1 Cubic Meter (l³)	≈	35.31 Cubic Feet (ft³)
1 Cubic Kilometer (km³)	≈	0.24 Cubic Miles (mi³)
0° Celsius (C)	≈	32° Fahrenheit (F)
100° Celsius (C)	≈	212° Fahrenheit (F)
1000° Celsius (C)	≈	1832° Fahrenheit (F)
2000° Celsius (C)	≈	3632° Fahrenheit (F)

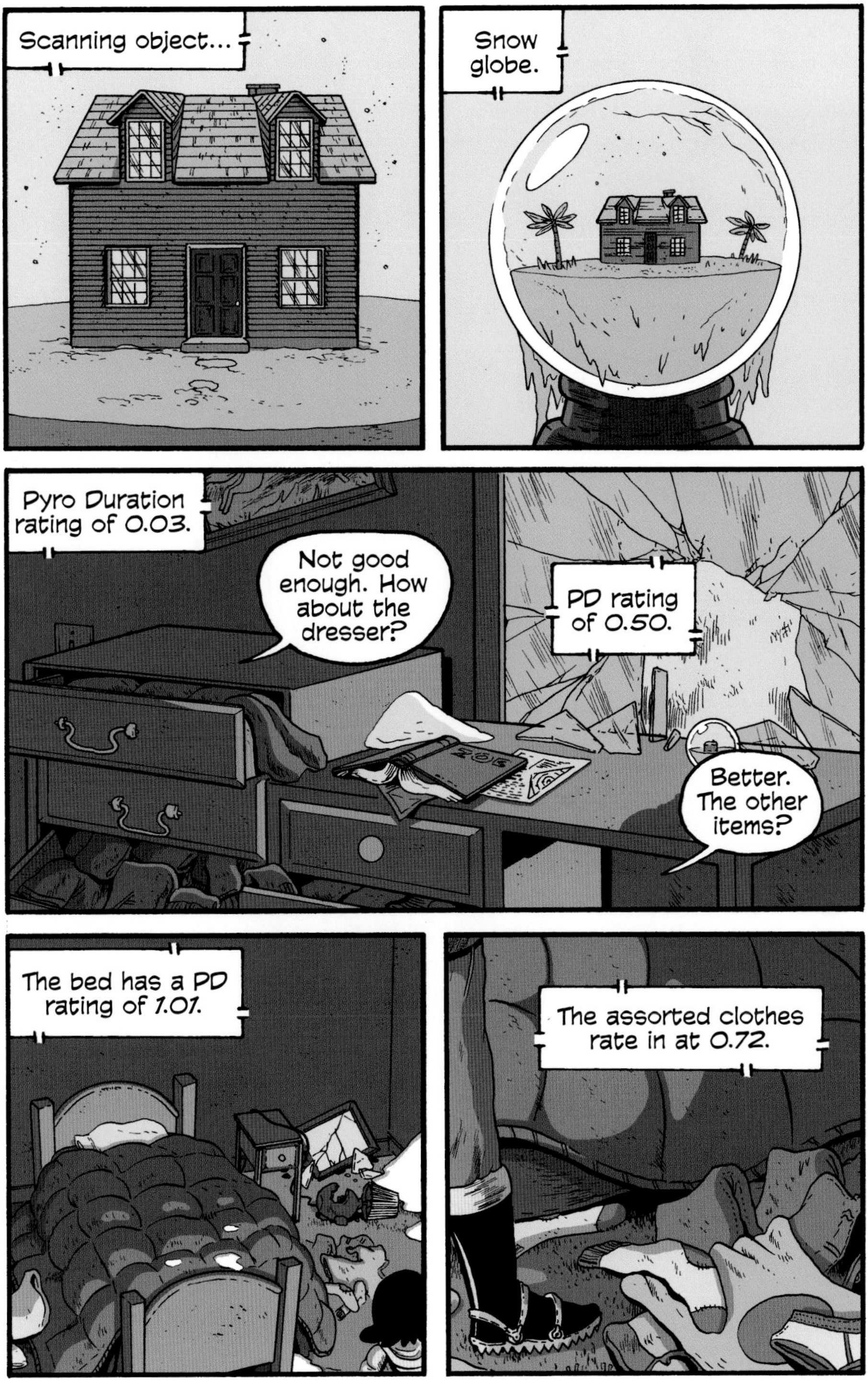
Scanning object...
Snow globe.
Pyro Duration rating of 0.03.
Not good enough. How about the dresser?
PD rating of 0.50.
Better. The other items?
The bed has a PD rating of 1.01.
The assorted clothes rate in at 0.72.

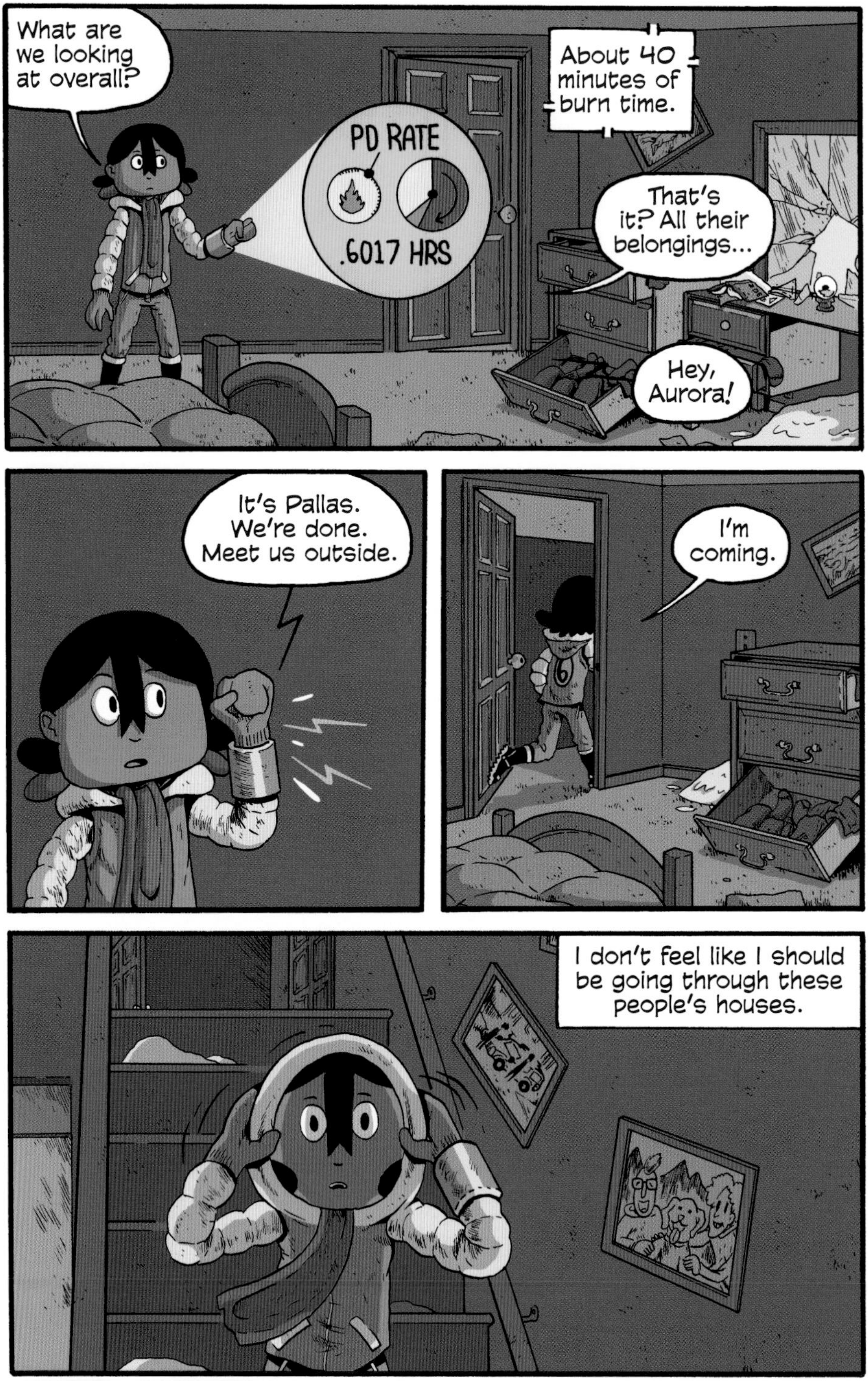
What are we looking at overall?
PD RATE
.6017 HRS
About 40 minutes of burn time.
That's it? All their belongings...
Hey, Aurora!
It's Pallas. We're done. Meet us outside.
I'm coming.
I don't feel like I should be going through these people's houses.

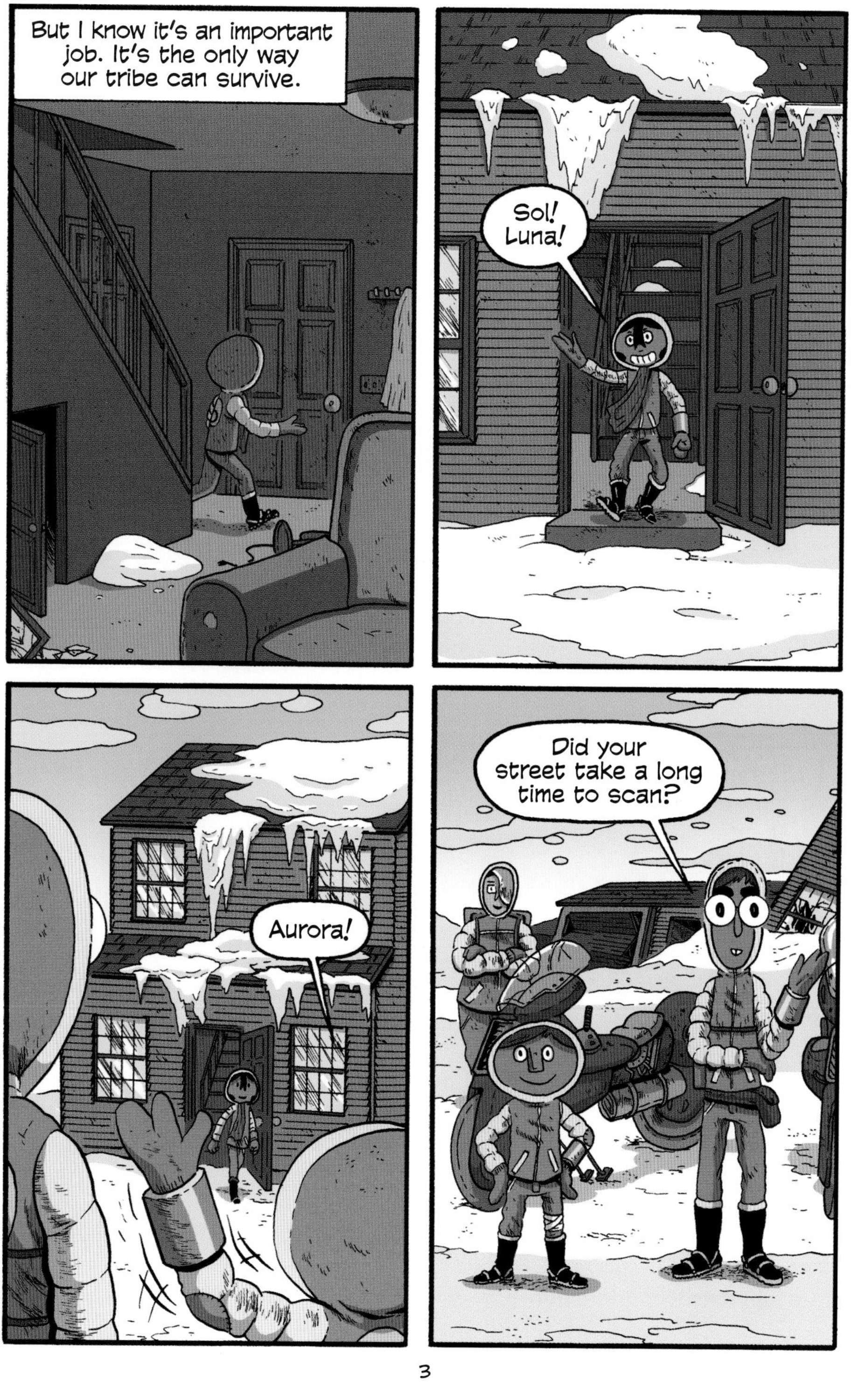
But I know it's an important job. It's the only way our tribe can survive.
Sol! Luna!
Aurora!
Did your street take a long time to scan?

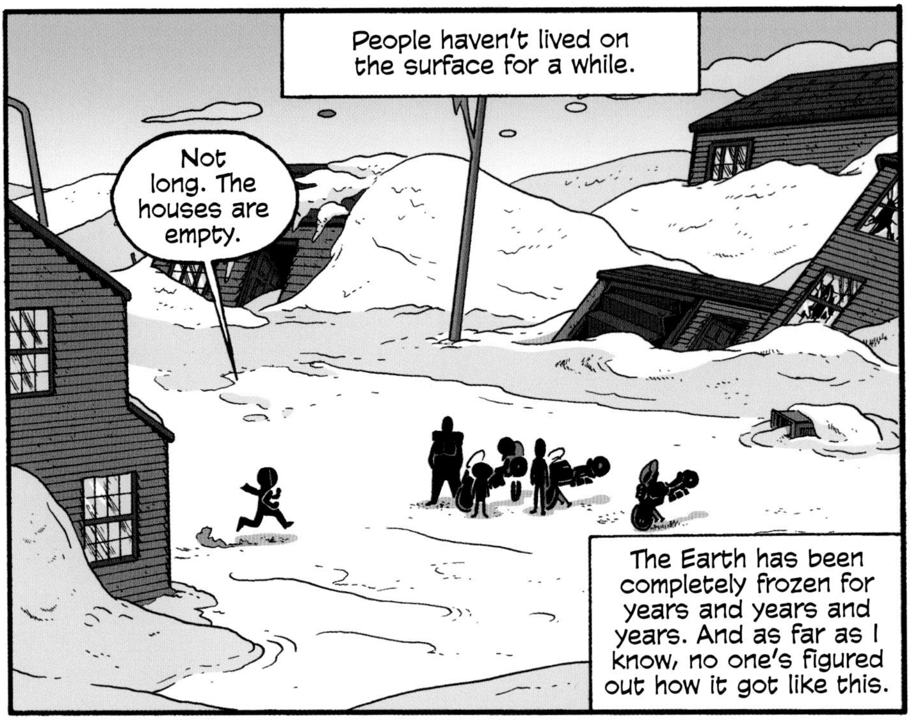
People haven't lived on the surface for a while.
Not long. The houses are empty.
The Earth has been completely frozen for years and years and years. And as far as I know, no one's figured out how it got like this.

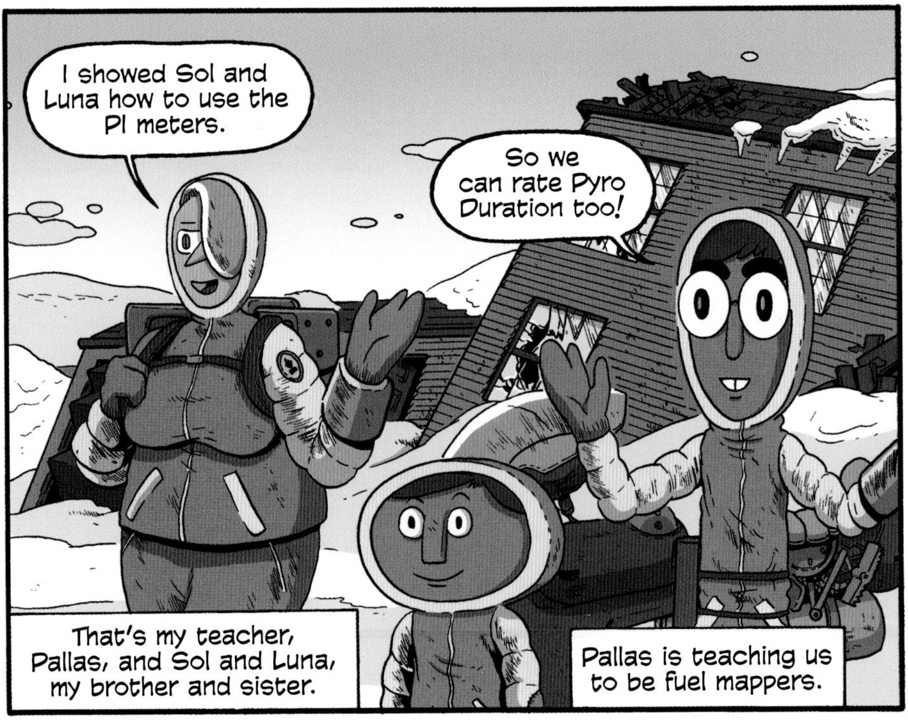
I showed Sol and Luna how to use the PI meters.
So we can rate Pyro Duration too!
That's my teacher, Pallas, and Sol and Luna, my brother and sister.
Pallas is teaching us to be fuel mappers.

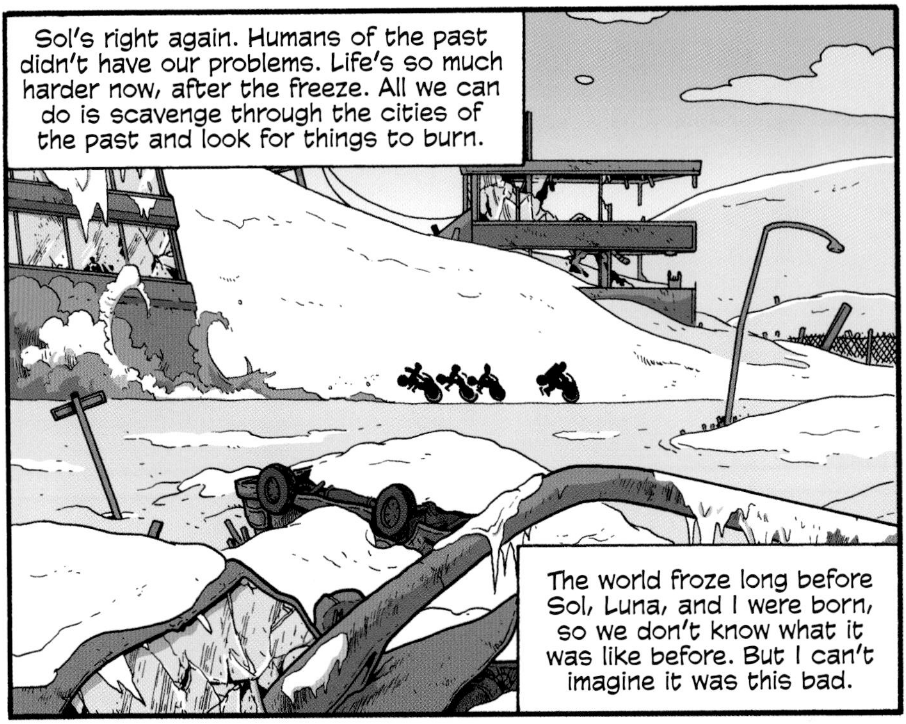
Sol's right again. Humans of the past didn't have our problems. Life's so much harder now, after the freeze. All we can do is scavenge through the cities of the past and look for things to burn.
The world froze long before Sol, Luna, and I were born, so we don't know what it was like before. But I can't imagine it was this bad.

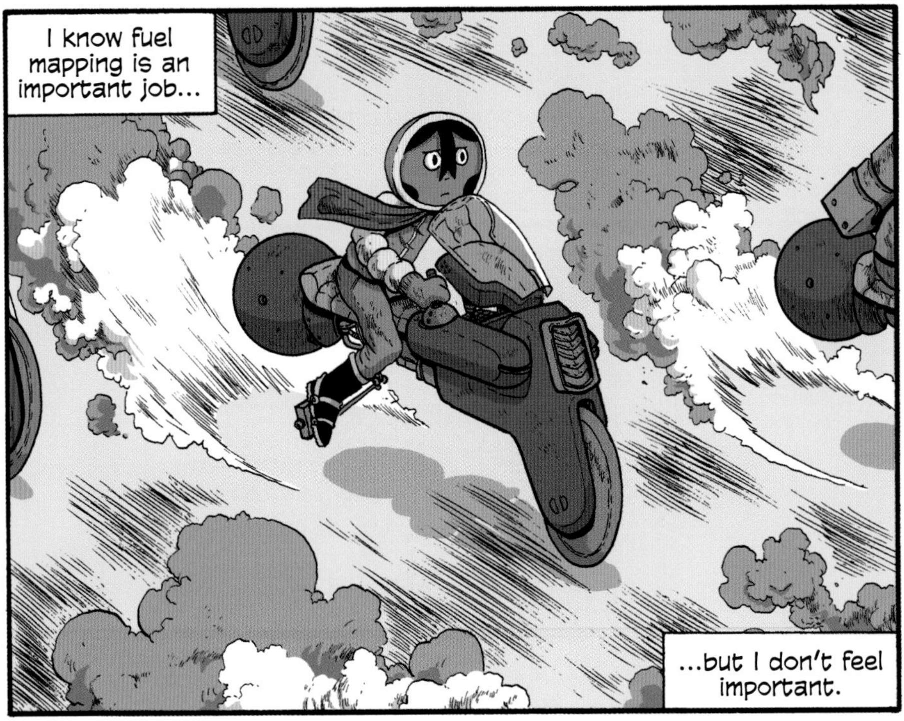
I know fuel mapping is an important job...
...but I don't feel important.

7

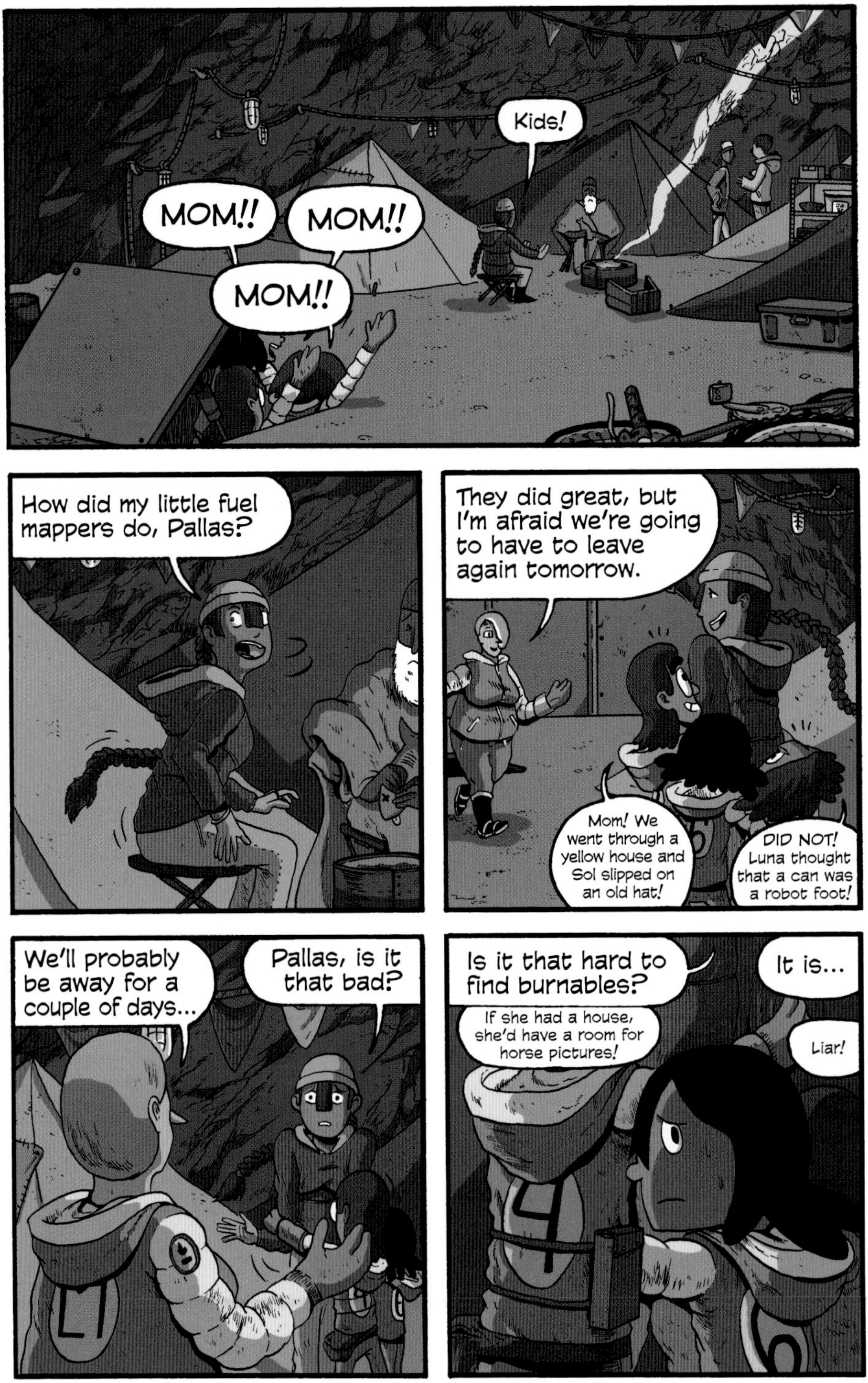
Kids!
MOM!!
MOM!!
MOM!!
How did my little fuel mappers do, Pallas?
They did great, but I'm afraid we're going to have to leave again tomorrow.
Mom! We went through a yellow house and Sol slipped on an old hat!
DID NOT! Luna thought that a can was a robot foot!
We'll probably be away for a couple of days...
Pallas, is it that bad?
Is it that hard to find burnables?
It is...
If she had a house, she'd have a room for horse pictures!
Liar!

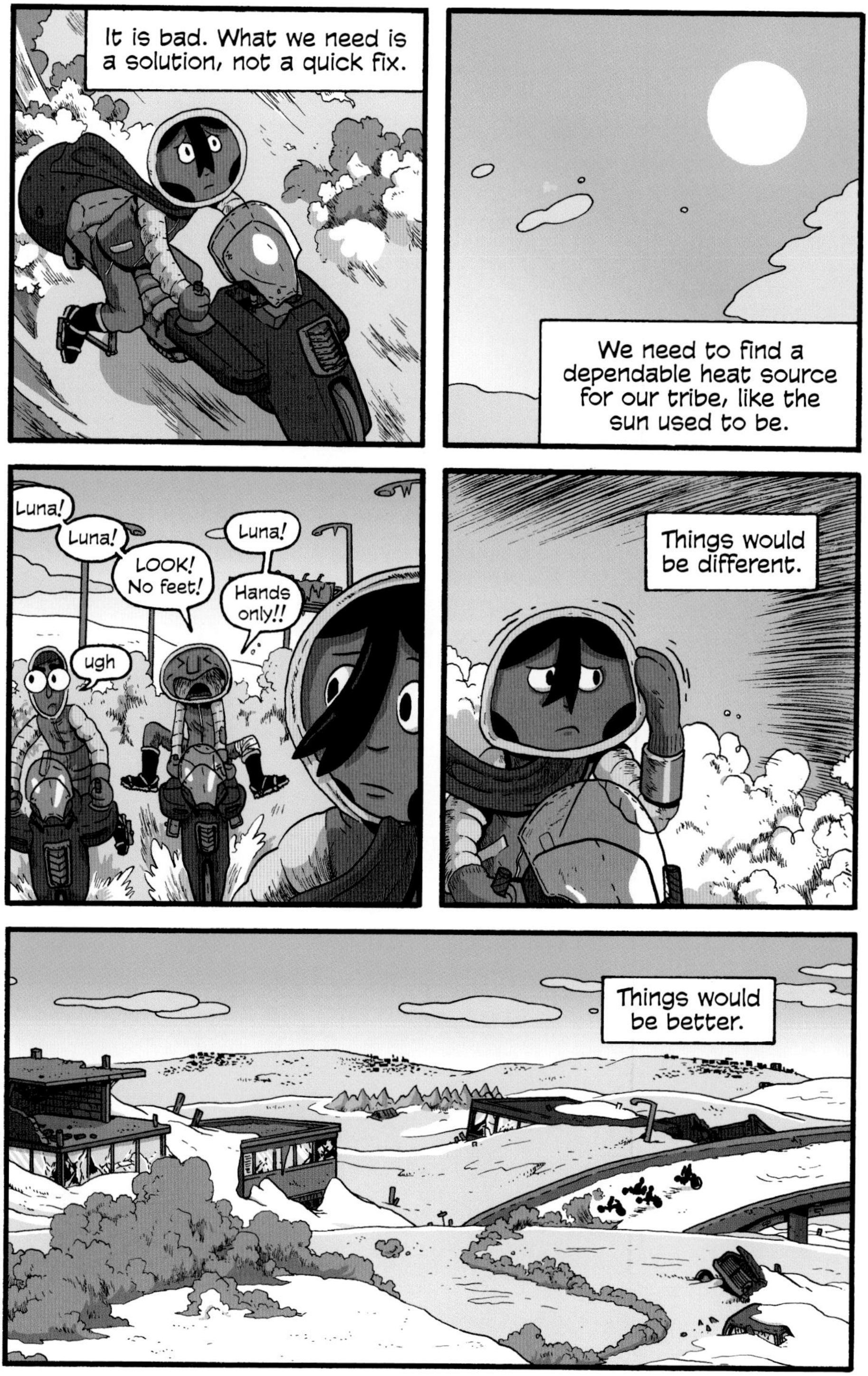
It is bad. What we need is a solution, not a quick fix.
We need to find a dependable heat source for our tribe, like the sun used to be.
Luna!
Luna!
LOOK! No feet!
Luna!
Hands only!!
ugh
Things would be different.
Things would be better.

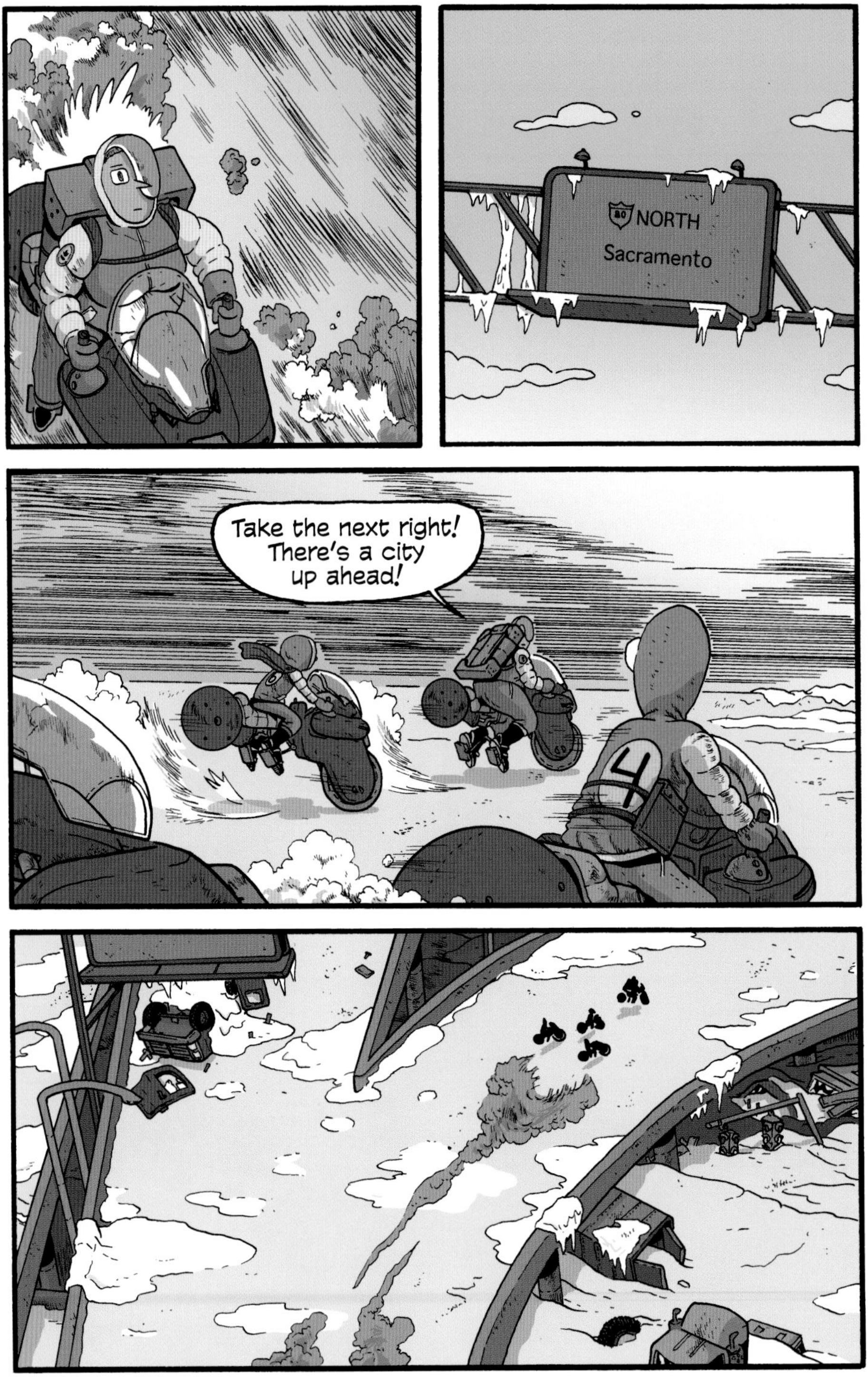
NORTH
Sacramento
Take the next right! There's a city up ahead!

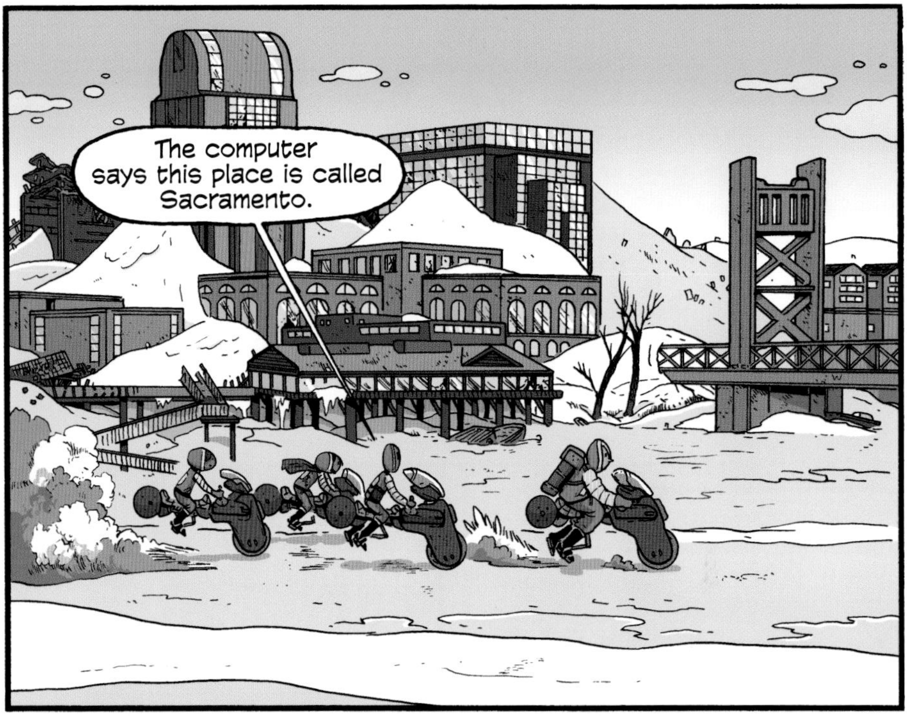
The computer says this place is called Sacramento.

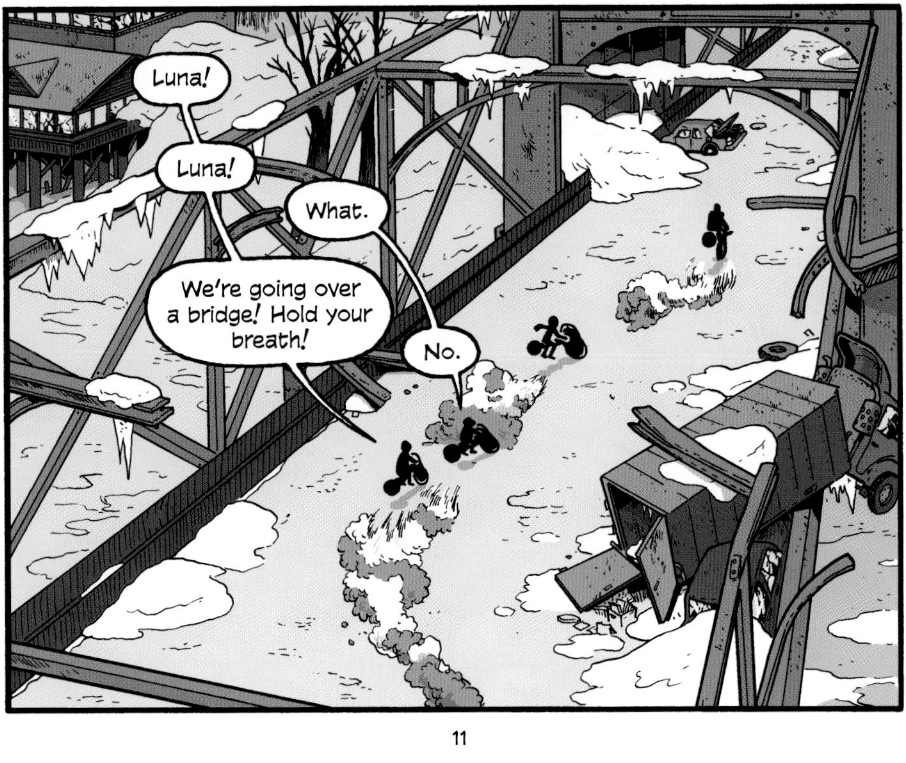
Luna!
Luna!
What.
We're going over a bridge! Hold your breath!
No.

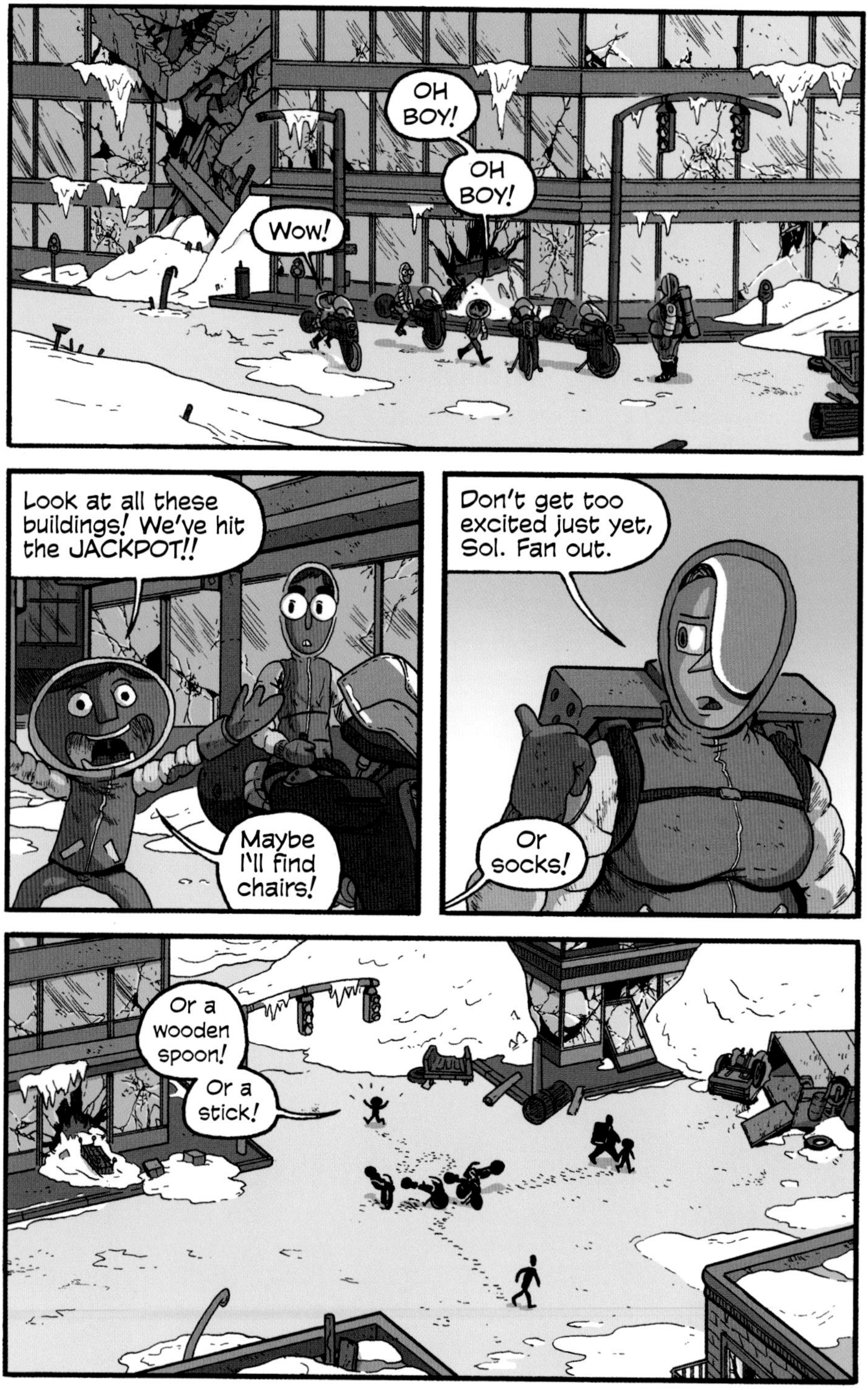
OH BOY!
OH BOY!
Wow!
Look at all these buildings! We've hit the JACKPOT!!
Maybe I'll find chairs!
Don't get too excited just yet, Sol. Fan out.
Or socks!
Or a wooden spoon!
Or a stick!

13

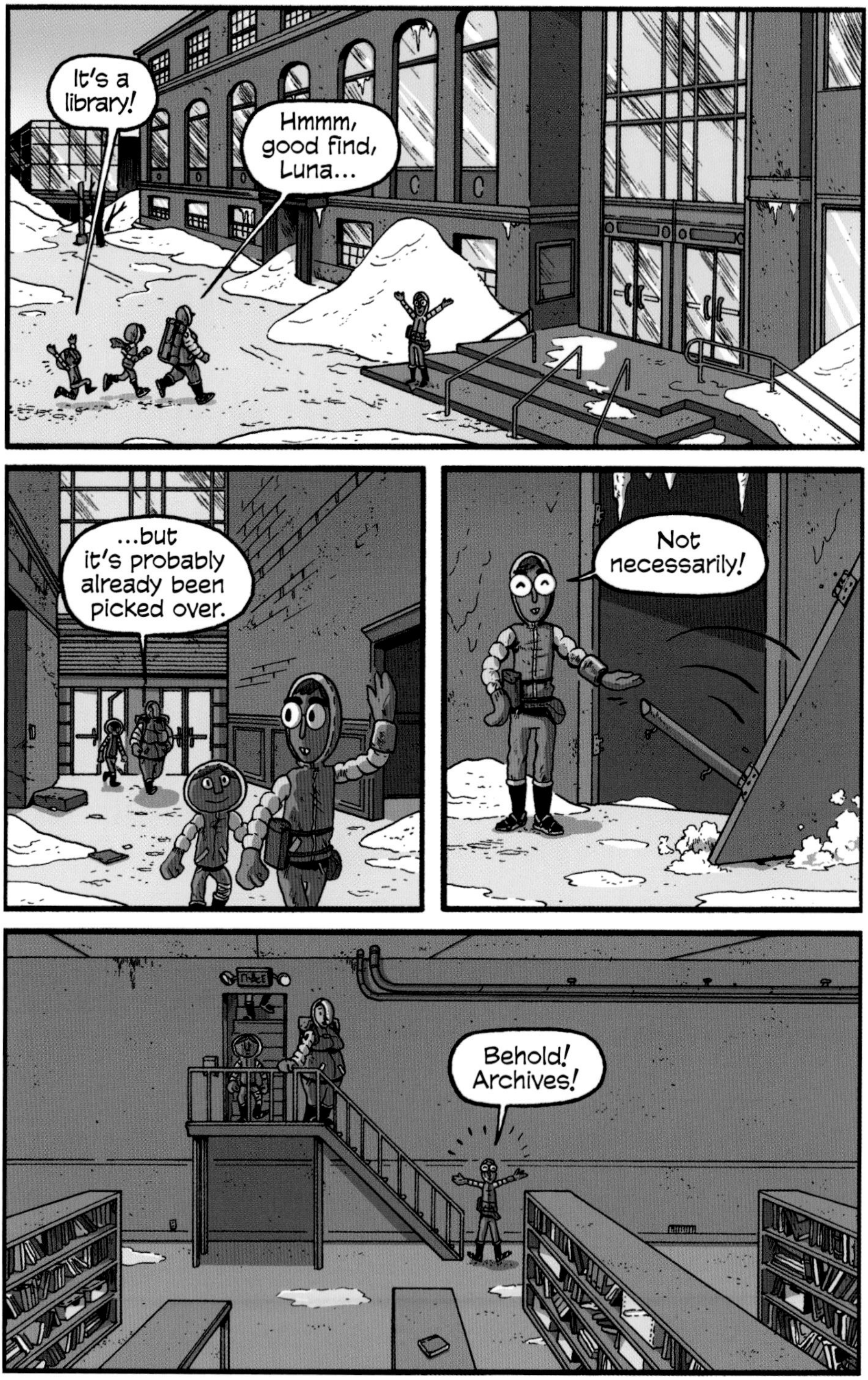
It's a library!
Hmmm, good find, Luna...
...but it's probably already been picked over.
Not necessarily!
Behold! Archives!

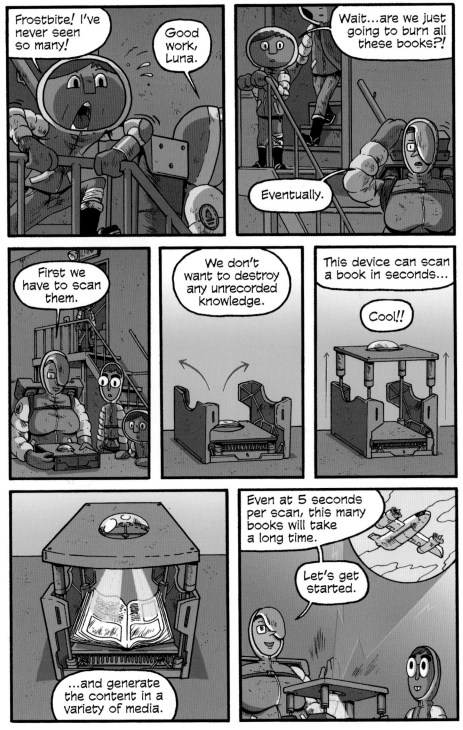

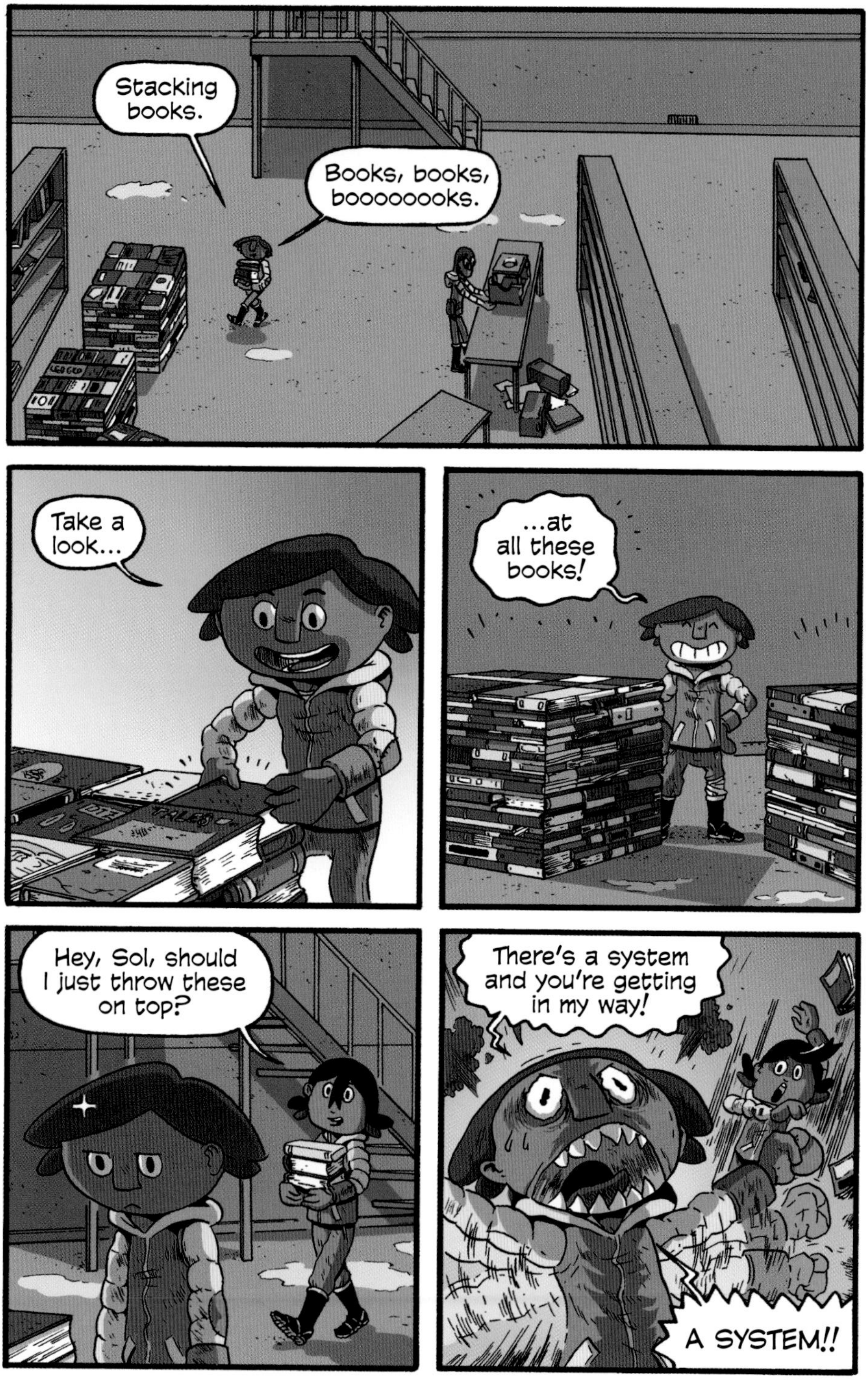
Stacking books.
Books, books, boooooooks.
Take a look...
...at all these books!
Hey, Sol, should I just throw these on top?
There's a system and you're getting in my way!
A SYSTEM!!

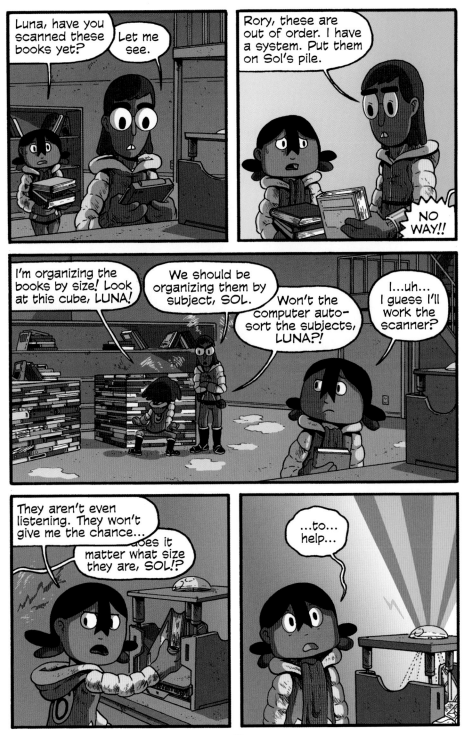

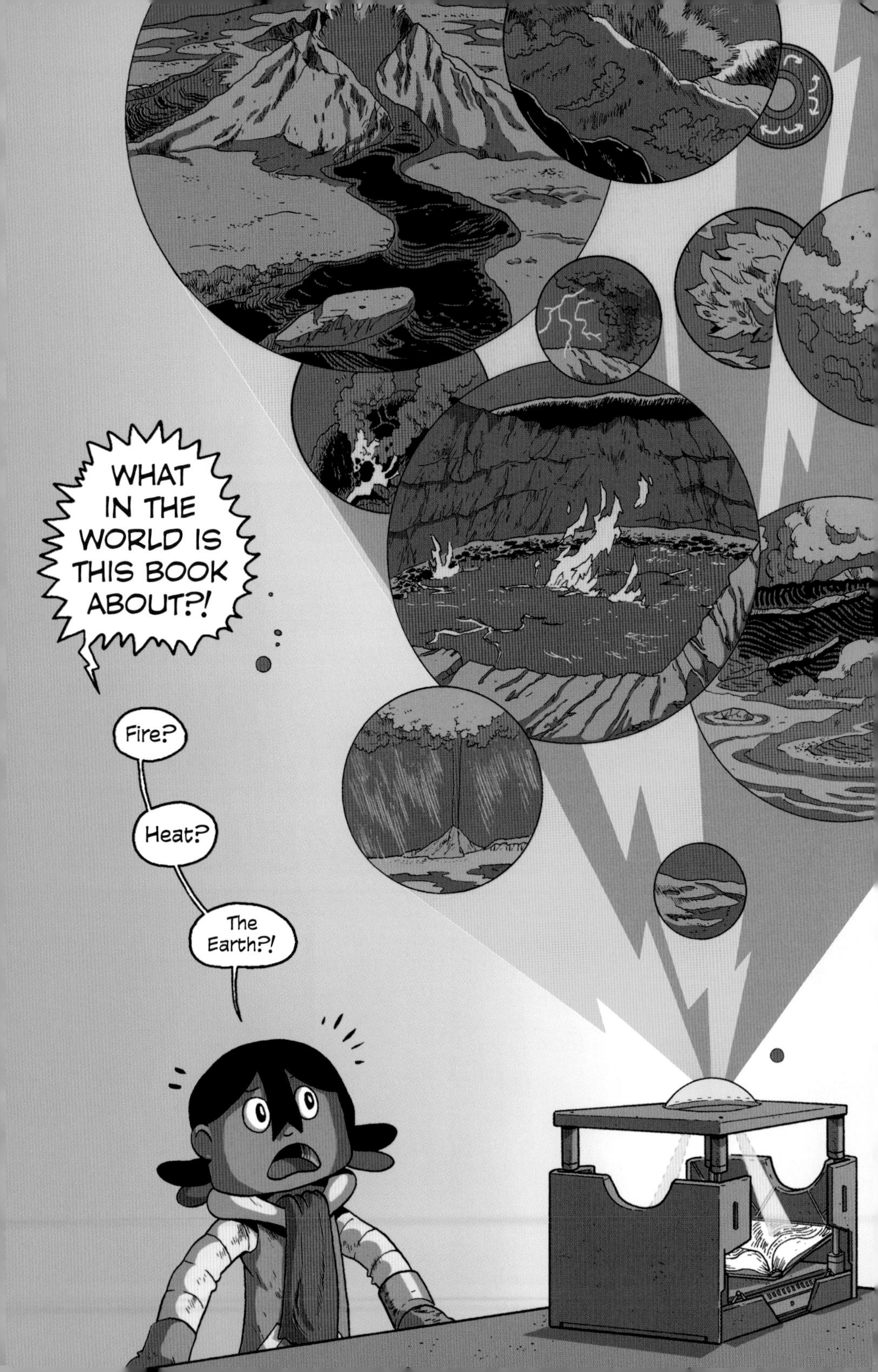
WHAT IN THE WORLD IS THIS BOOK ABOUT?!
Fire?
Heat?
The Earth?!

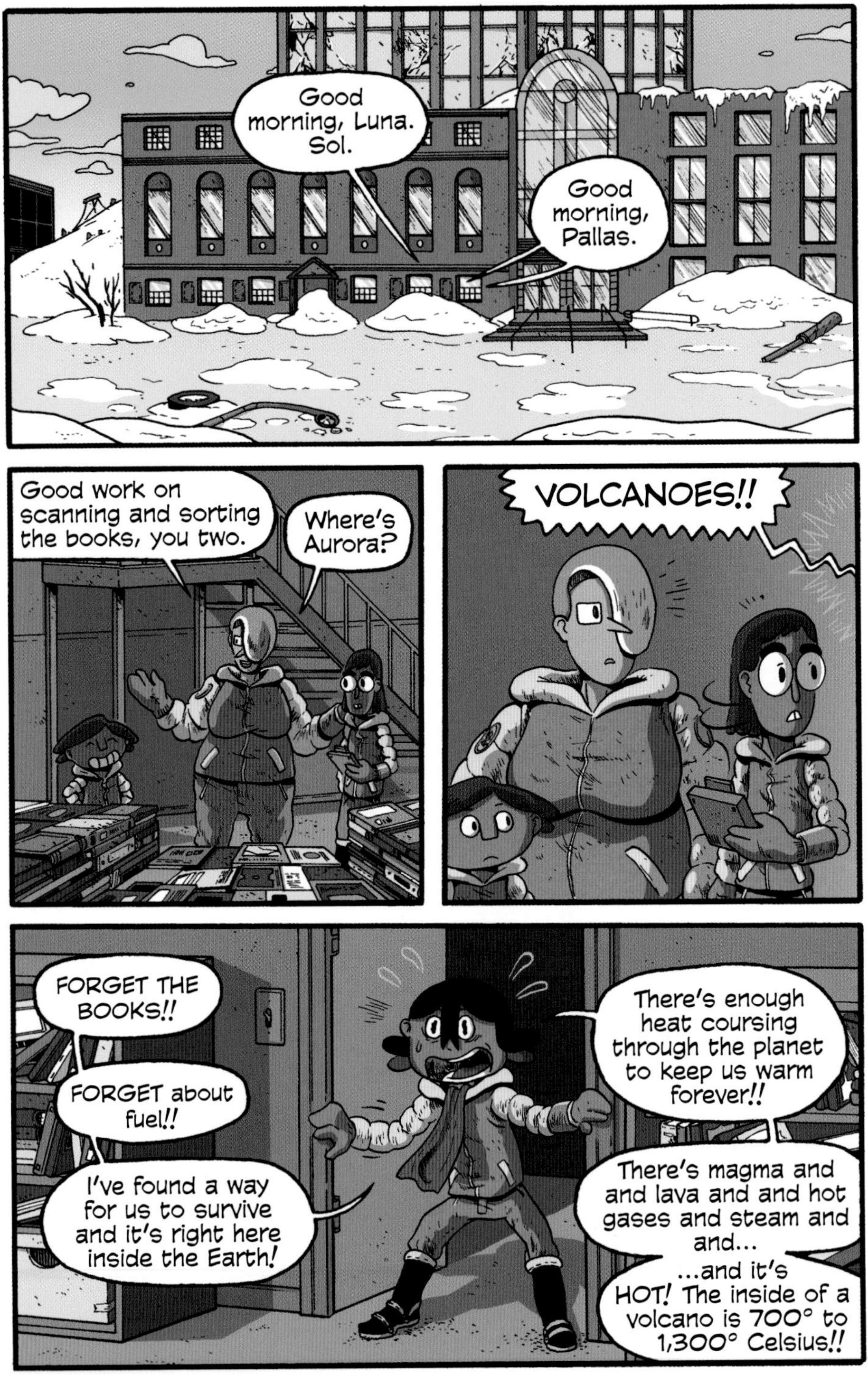
Good morning, Luna. Sol.
Good morning, Pallas.
Good work on scanning and sorting the books, you two.
Where's Aurora?
VOLCANOES!!
FORGET THE BOOKS!!
FORGET about fuel!!
I've found a way for us to survive and it's right here inside the Earth!
There's enough heat coursing through the planet to keep us warm forever!!
There's magma and and lava and and hot gases and steam and and...
...and it's HOT! The inside of a volcano is 700° to 1,300° Celsius!!

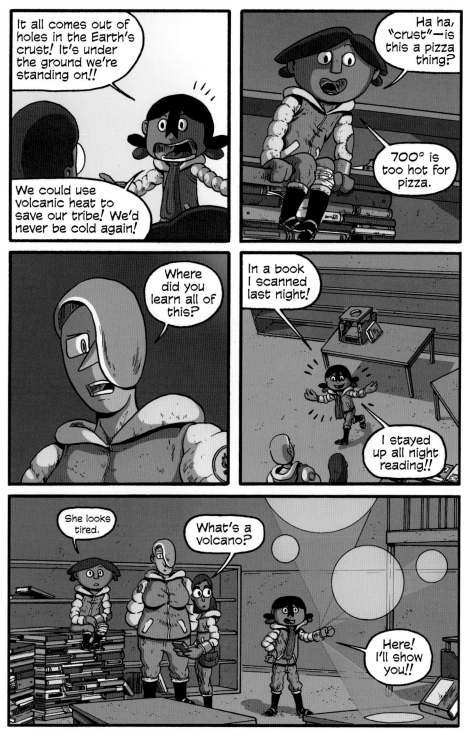

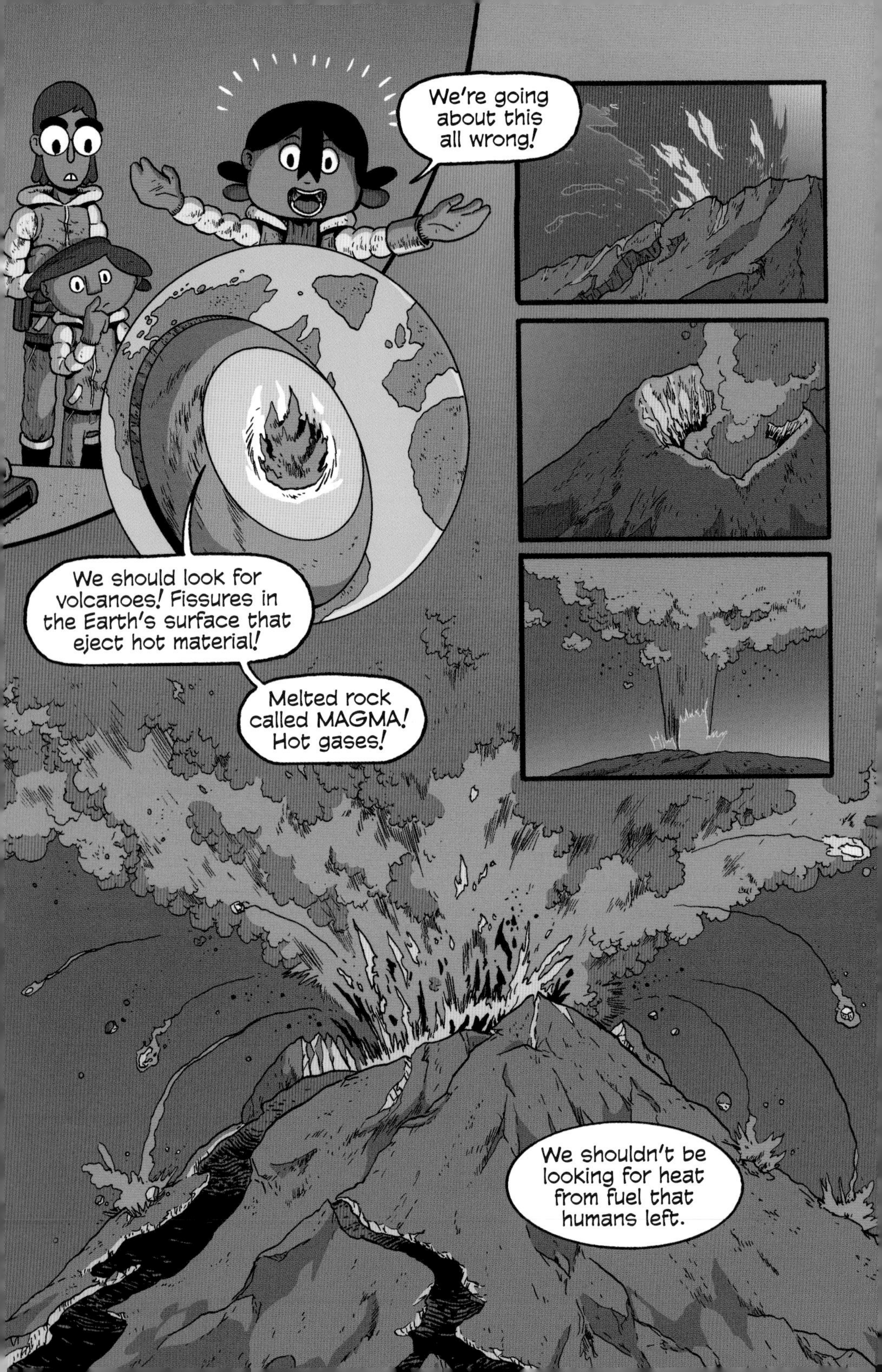
We're going about this all wrong!
We should look for volcanoes! Fissures in the Earth's surface that eject hot material!
Melted rock called MAGMA! Hot gases!
We shouldn't be looking for heat from fuel that humans left.

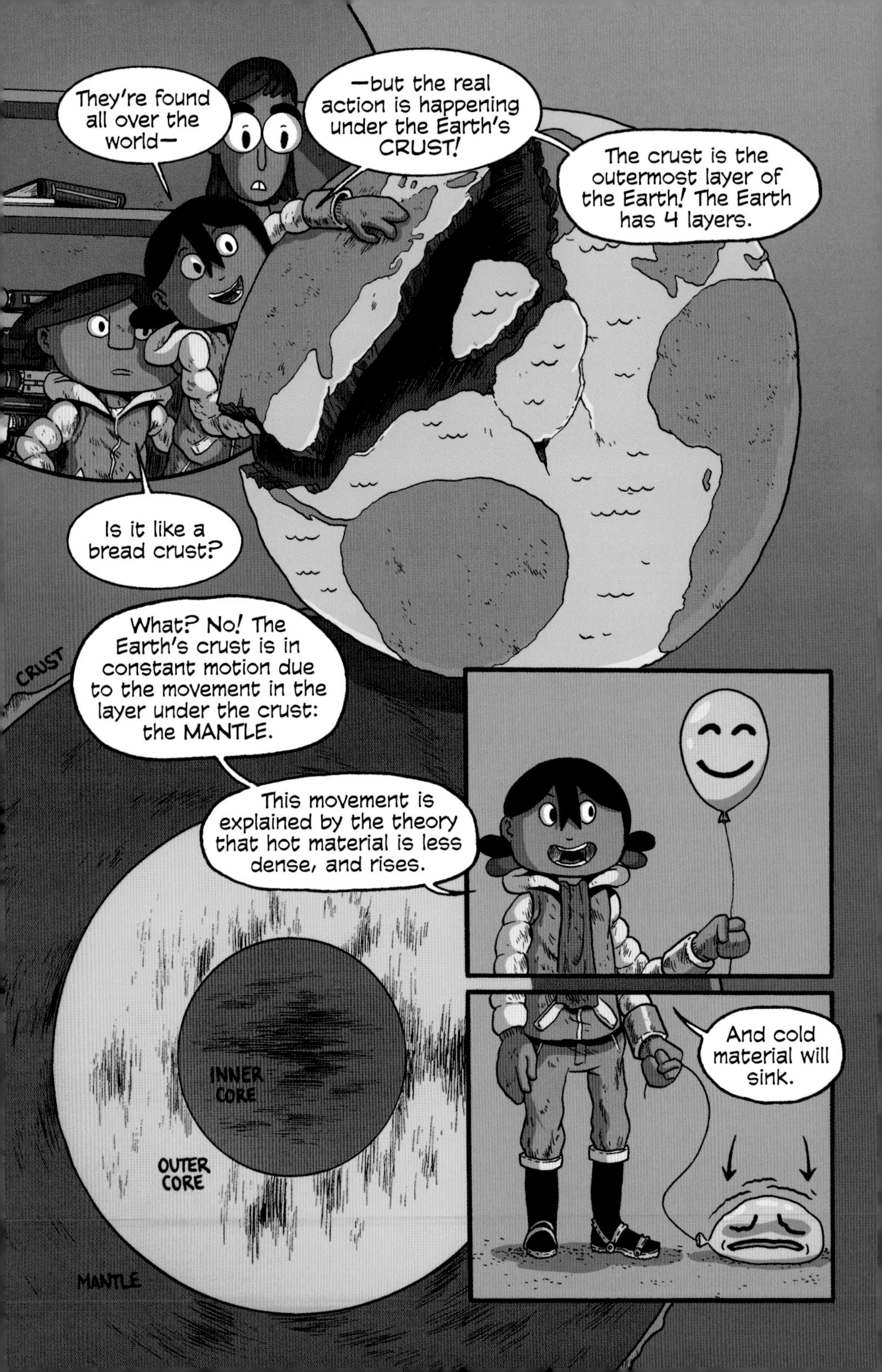
They're found all over the world—
—but the real action is happening under the Earth's CRUST!
The crust is the outermost layer of the Earth! The Earth has 4 layers.
Is it like a bread crust?
What? No! The Earth's crust is in constant motion due to the movement in the layer under the crust: the MANTLE.
CRUST
This movement is explained by the theory that hot material is less dense, and rises.
INNER CORE
OUTER CORE
MANTLE
And cold material will sink.

The mantle is made of hot, flexible rock.

Even though it's solid, the way the hotter sections of the mantle rise and the cooler parts sink creates a current—

—and this moves OCEANIC and CONTINENTAL plates toward and away from each other.

NOT AS HOT

NOT AS HOT

HOT

HOT

When two plates move toward each other, it is called a CONVERGENT BOUNDARY.

The heavier, denser plate will descend, or SUBDUCT, under the less dense plate.

When an oceanic plate subducts under another oceanic plate—

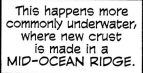

—the result is an ISLAND ARC.

When an oceanic plate subducts under a continental plate—

—the result is a volcano on the surface.

When two plates move AWAY from each other, it is called a DIVERGENT BOUNDARY.

This happens more commonly underwater, where new crust is made in a MID-OCEAN RIDGE.

The only two divergent boundaries on dry land run through Iceland and the Rift Valley of East Africa.

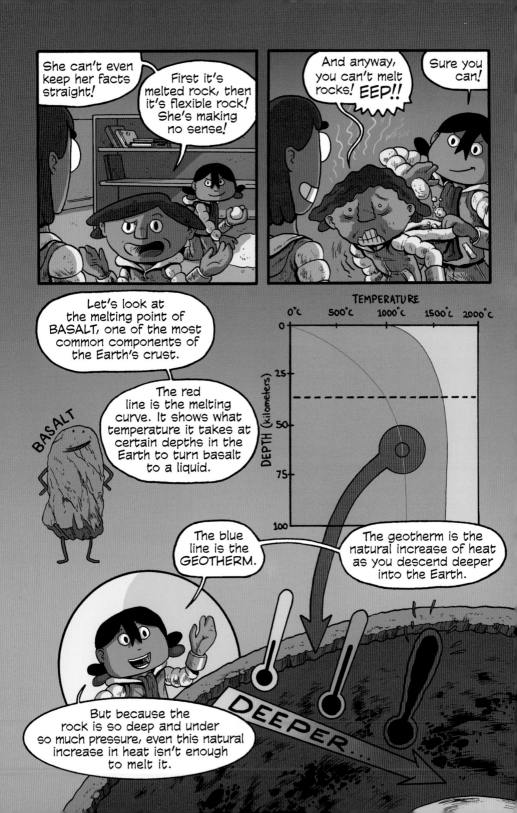

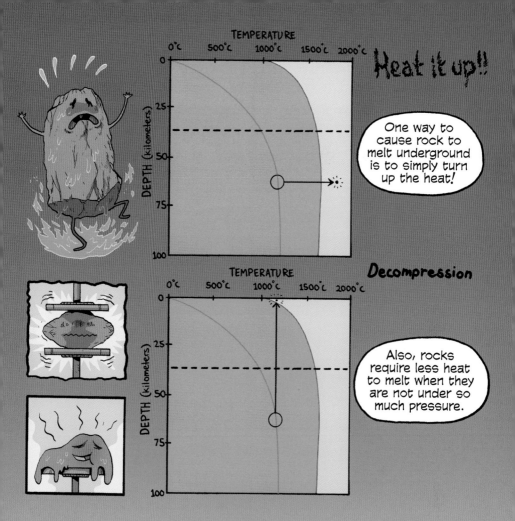

Heat it up!!

One way to cause rock to melt underground is to simply turn up the heat!

Decompression

Also, rocks require less heat to melt when they are not under so much pressure.

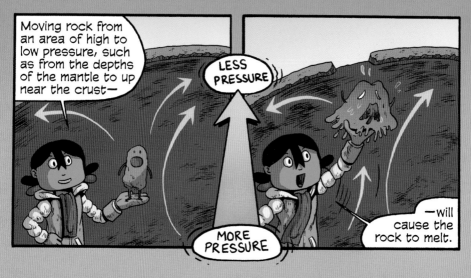

Moving rock from an area of high to low pressure, such as from the depths of the mantle to up near the crust—

LESS PRESSURE

MORE PRESSURE

—will cause the rock to melt.

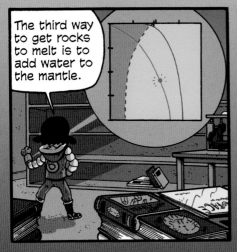

The third way to get rocks to melt is to add water to the mantle.

But wouldn't water evaporate if it is so hot?

Yes!

OCEANIC

CONTINENTAL

COLD, WET

Let's look at this CONVERGENT BOUNDARY. The oceanic crust is subducting under the continental crust.

Compared to the mantle, the Earth's crust is cold, and it contains water.

Woo-hoo! Going down!

It holds water like a sponge?

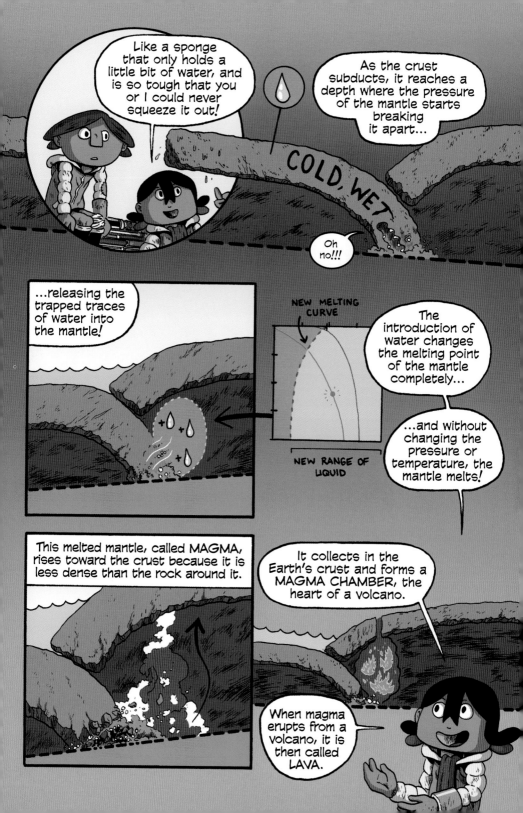

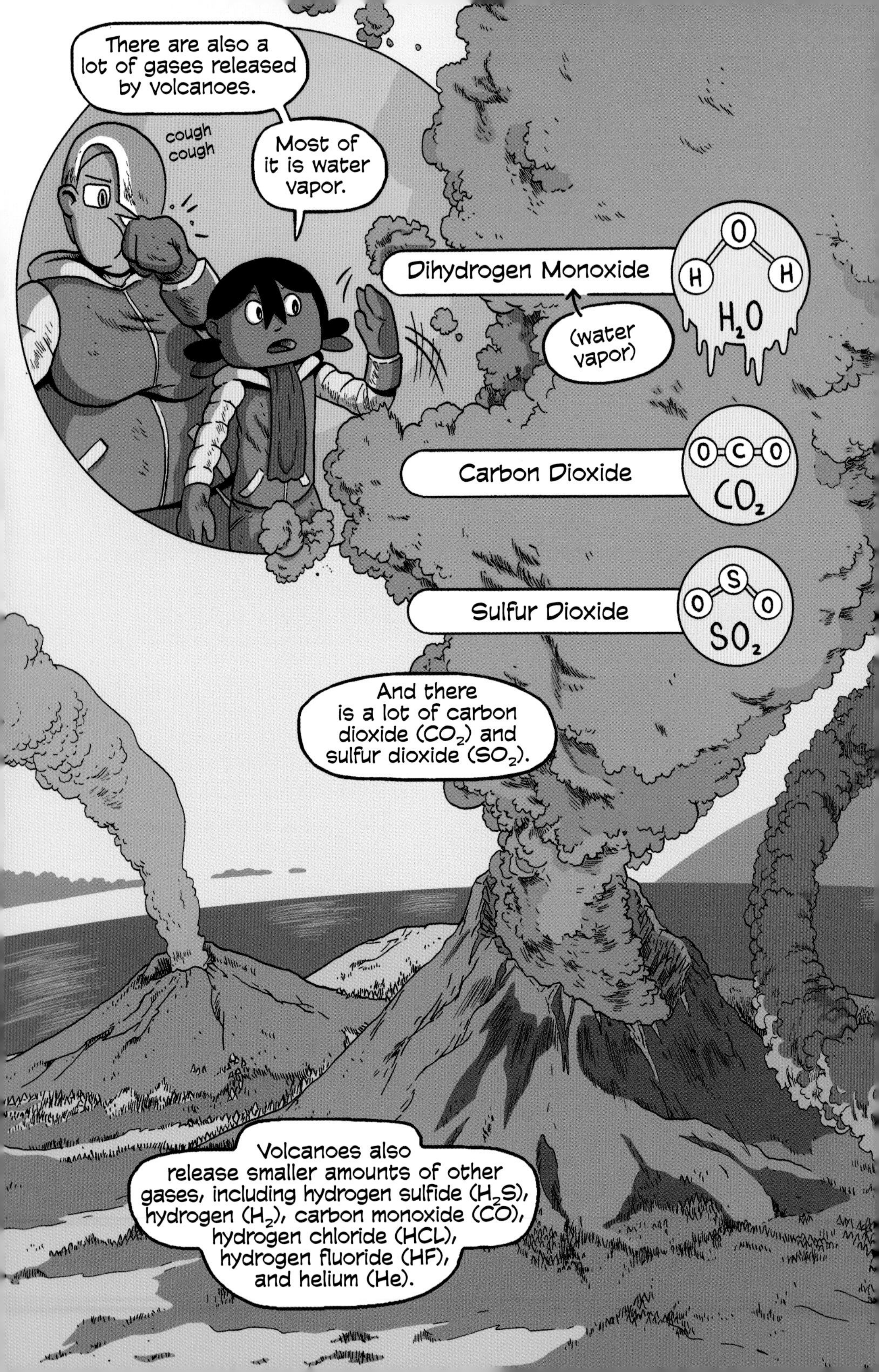

There are also a lot of gases released by volcanoes.
cough cough
Most of it is water vapor.
Dihydrogen Monoxide
(water vapor)
H_2O
Carbon Dioxide
CO_2
Sulfur Dioxide
SO_2
And there is a lot of carbon dioxide (CO_2) and sulfur dioxide (SO_2).
Volcanoes also release smaller amounts of other gases, including hydrogen sulfide (H_2S), hydrogen (H_2), carbon monoxide (CO), hydrogen chloride (HCL), hydrogen fluoride (HF), and helium (He).

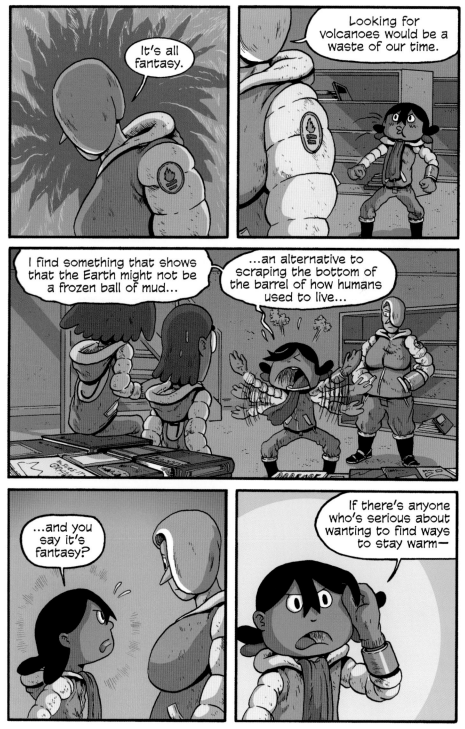

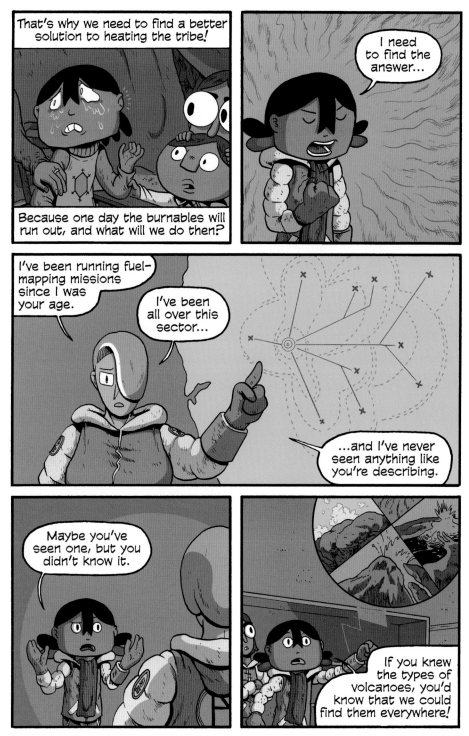

That's why we need to find a better solution to heating the tribe!

Because one day the burnables will run out, and what will we do then?

I need to find the answer...

I've been running fuel-mapping missions since I was your age.

I've been all over this sector...

...and I've never seen anything like you're describing.

Maybe you've seen one, but you didn't know it.

If you knew the types of volcanoes, you'd know that we could find them everywhere!

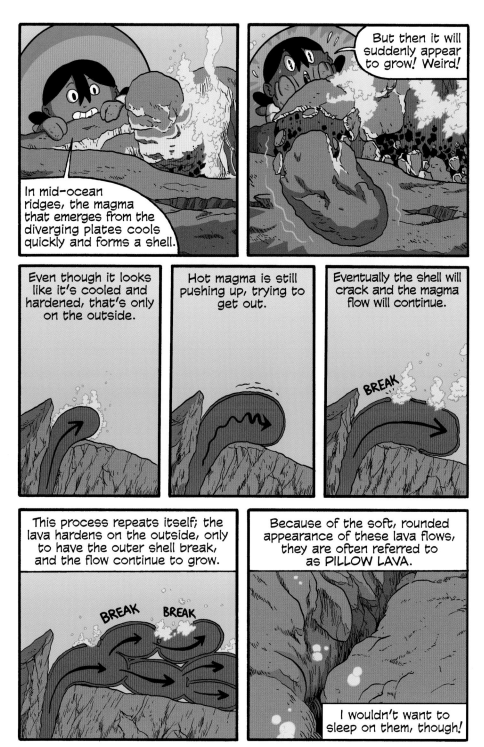

39

When pressure builds up in the magma chamber, the "cork" of volcanic material packed into the crater explodes outward.

As the liquid rock flies through the air, it cools and breaks into smaller pieces.

The erupted cinders, rocks, and lava stack up on the sides of the cinder cone in layers, building it up over hundreds of thousands of years! Like snow building up on a hill, layer after layer, snowfall after snowfall.

It's always about food with you...

Oh, "cone" like an ice-cream cone, right?

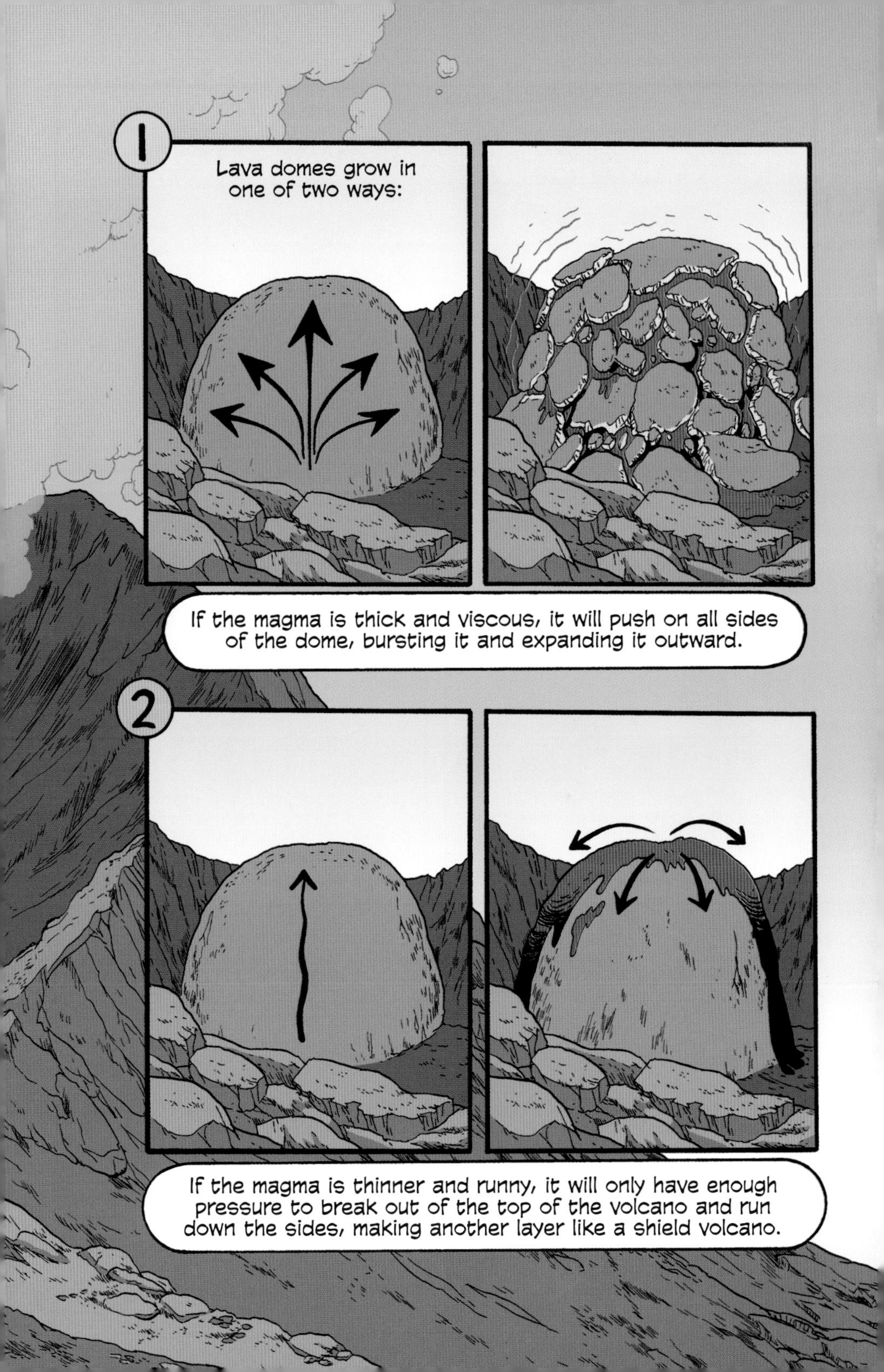
1
Lava domes grow in one of two ways:
If the magma is thick and viscous, it will push on all sides of the dome, bursting it and expanding it outward.
2
If the magma is thinner and runny, it will only have enough pressure to break out of the top of the volcano and run down the sides, making another layer like a shield volcano.

49

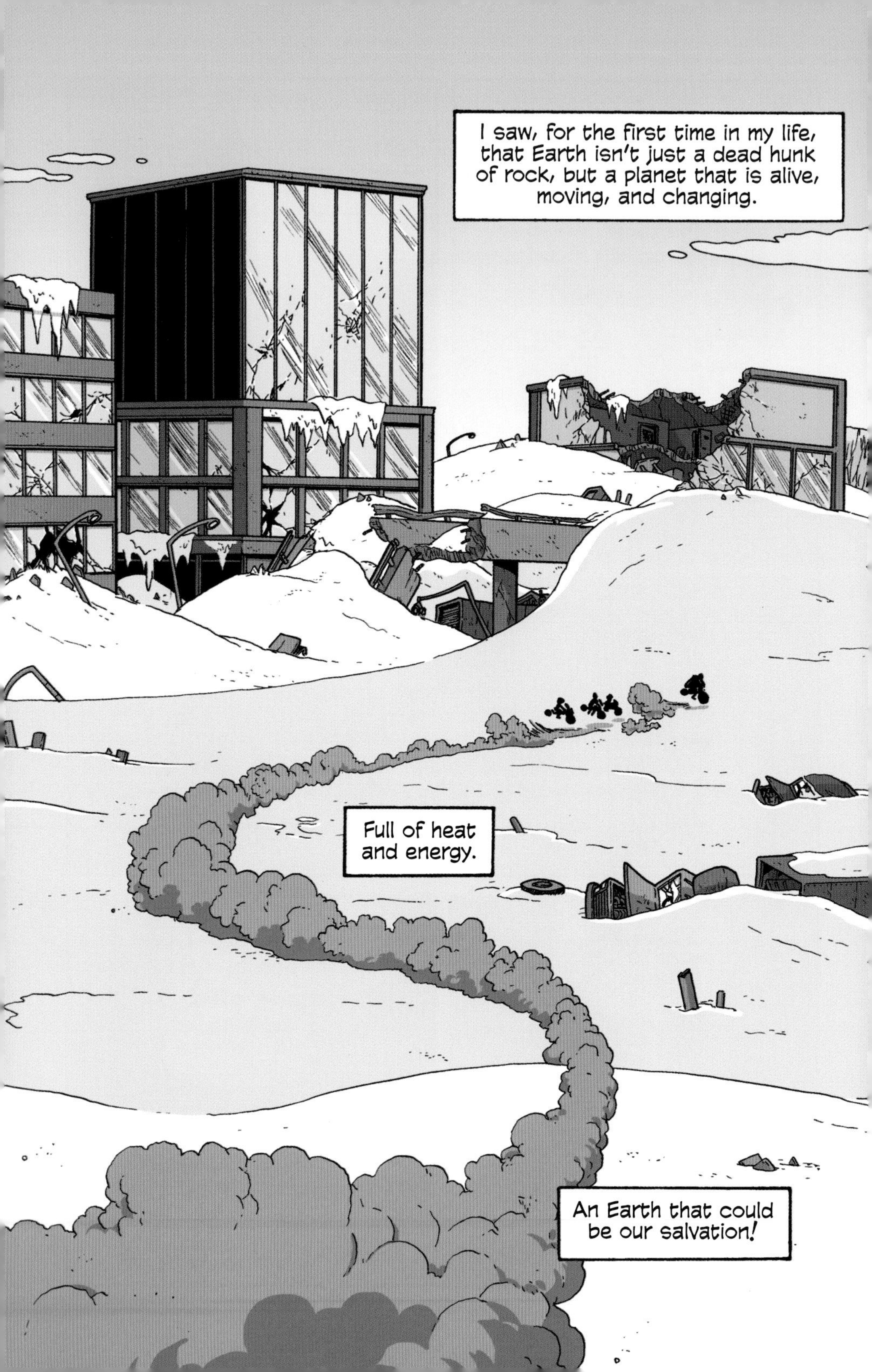
I saw, for the first time in my life, that Earth isn't just a dead hunk of rock, but a planet that is alive, moving, and changing.
Full of heat and energy.
An Earth that could be our salvation!

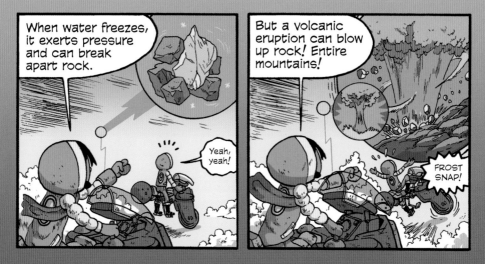

When water freezes, it exerts pressure and can break apart rock.

Yeah, yeah!

But a volcanic eruption can blow up rock! Entire mountains!

FROST SNAP!

The two main variables that will determine the strength and type of an eruption will be the viscosity of the magma...

1

THINNER
(MAFIC)

THICKER
(FELSIC)

2

...and the amount of gas in the magma.

POP

POP

When the rock is molten, the pressure is so great that the gasses are dissolved completely into the rock. Think of a soda bottle before you open it. There is CO_2 in the soda, but the bubbles aren't visible because they're under pressure.

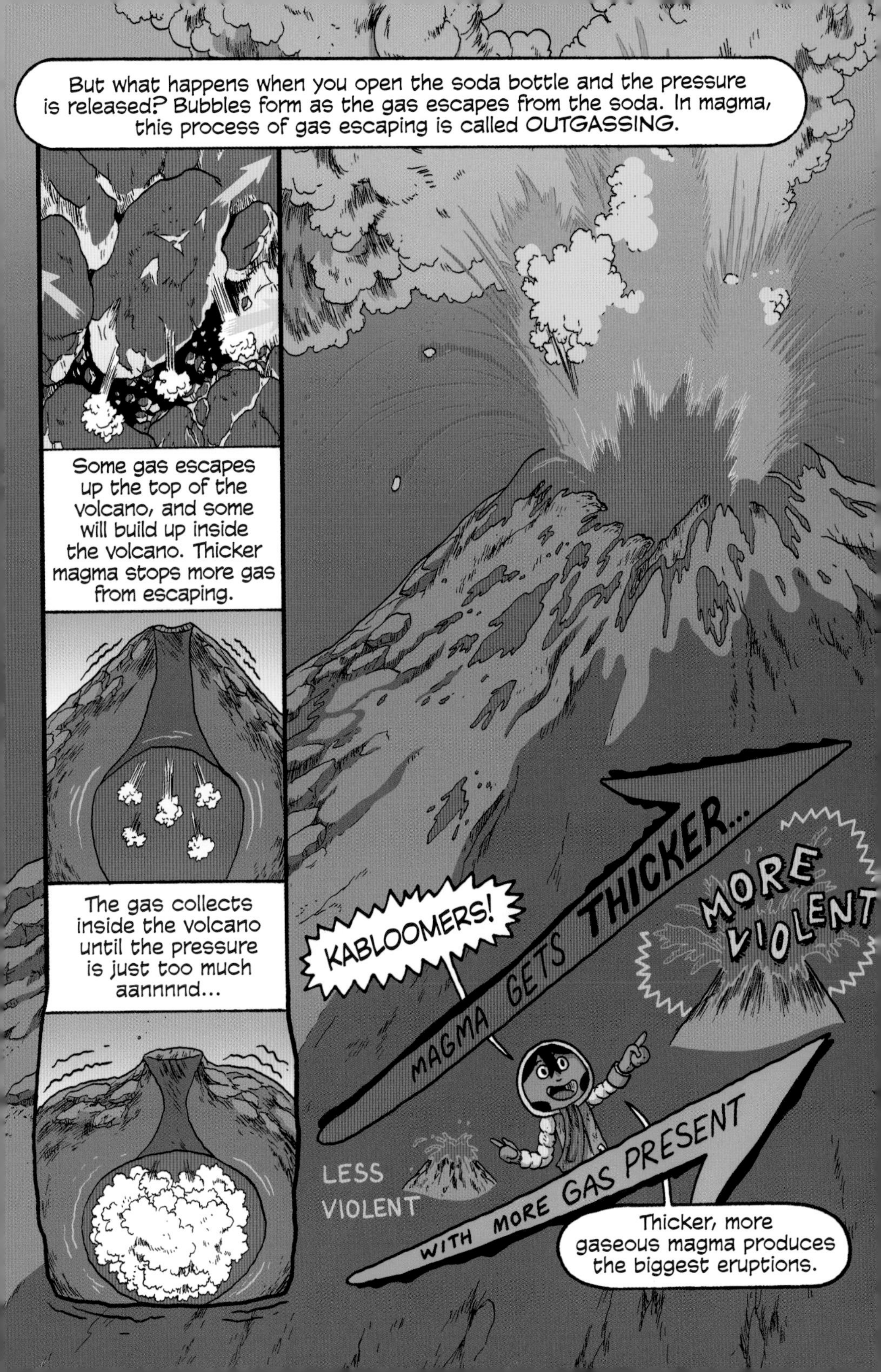
But what happens when you open the soda bottle and the pressure is released? Bubbles form as the gas escapes from the soda. In magma, this process of gas escaping is called OUTGASSING.
Some gas escapes up the top of the volcano, and some will build up inside the volcano. Thicker magma stops more gas from escaping.
The gas collects inside the volcano until the pressure is just too much aannnnd...
KABLOOMERS!
MAGMA GETS THICKER...
MORE VIOLENT
WITH MORE GAS PRESENT
LESS VIOLENT
Thicker, more gaseous magma produces the biggest eruptions.

One of the gentlest types of volcanic eruptions is a HAWAIIAN eruption.
Named for the volcanoes of the state of Hawaii, these eruptions are by comparison very calm.
500 meters
The lava that comes out of a Hawaiian eruption is typically more mafic, so it is very thin and runny.
Although there are some Hawaiian eruptions that can create a lava fountain 500 meters tall!

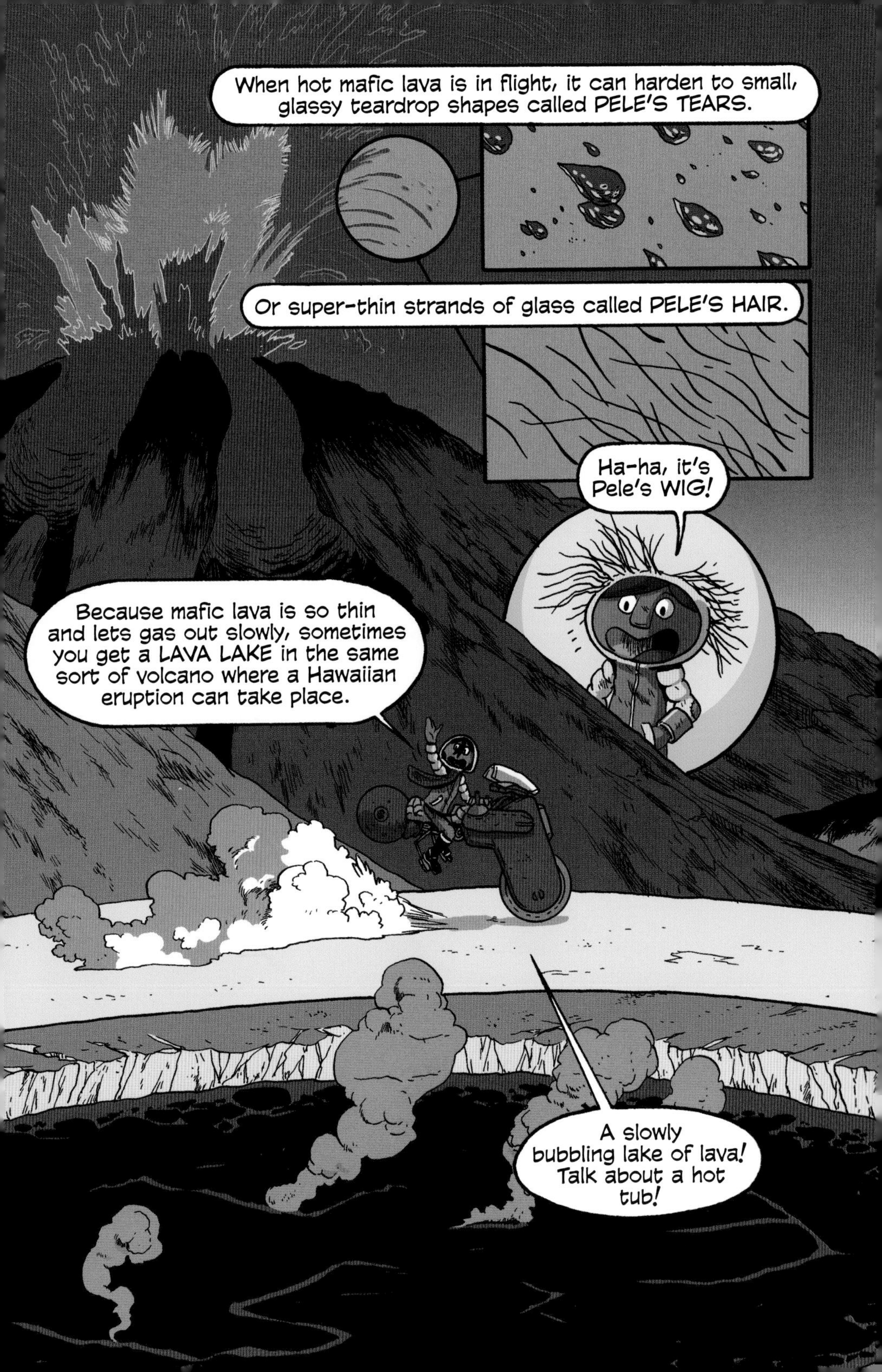
When hot mafic lava is in flight, it can harden to small, glassy teardrop shapes called PELE'S TEARS.
Or super-thin strands of glass called PELE'S HAIR.
Ha-ha, it's Pele's WIG!
Because mafic lava is so thin and lets gas out slowly, sometimes you get a LAVA LAKE in the same sort of volcano where a Hawaiian eruption can take place.
A slowly bubbling lake of lava! Talk about a hot tub!

An eruption that is a bit more volatile is a STROMBOLIAN eruption.
It's named after the volcano Stromboli, off the coast of Italy.
Stromboli has been active consistantly for over 2,000 years.
Its nickname is the Lighthouse of the Mediterranean!
From what you're saying, a more violent eruption is due to more gas in the magma and the magma being thicker?
That's right!
A little of both!

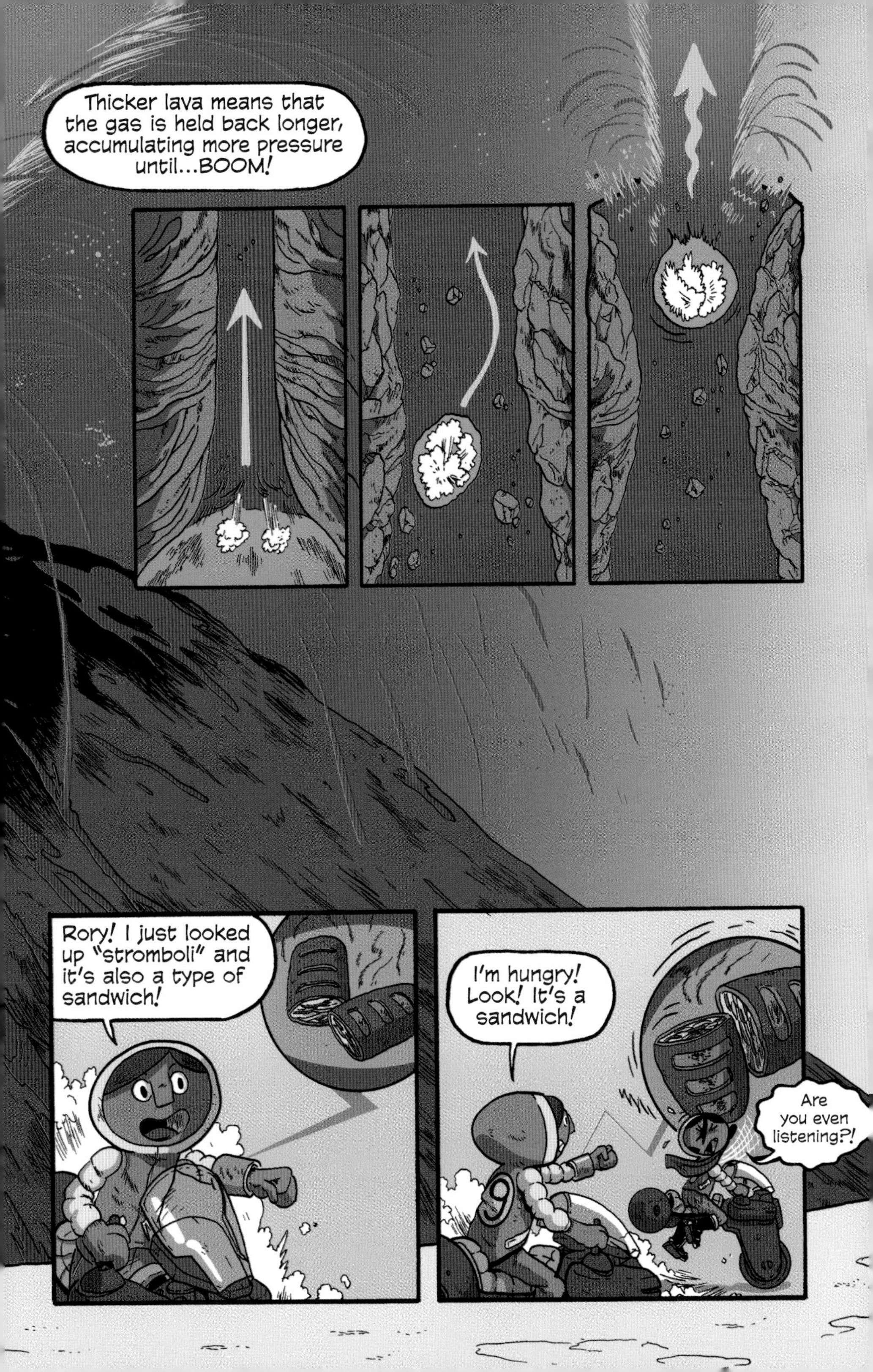
Thicker lava means that the gas is held back longer, accumulating more pressure until...BOOM!
Rory! I just looked up "stromboli" and it's also a type of sandwich!
I'm hungry! Look! It's a sandwich!
Are you even listening?!

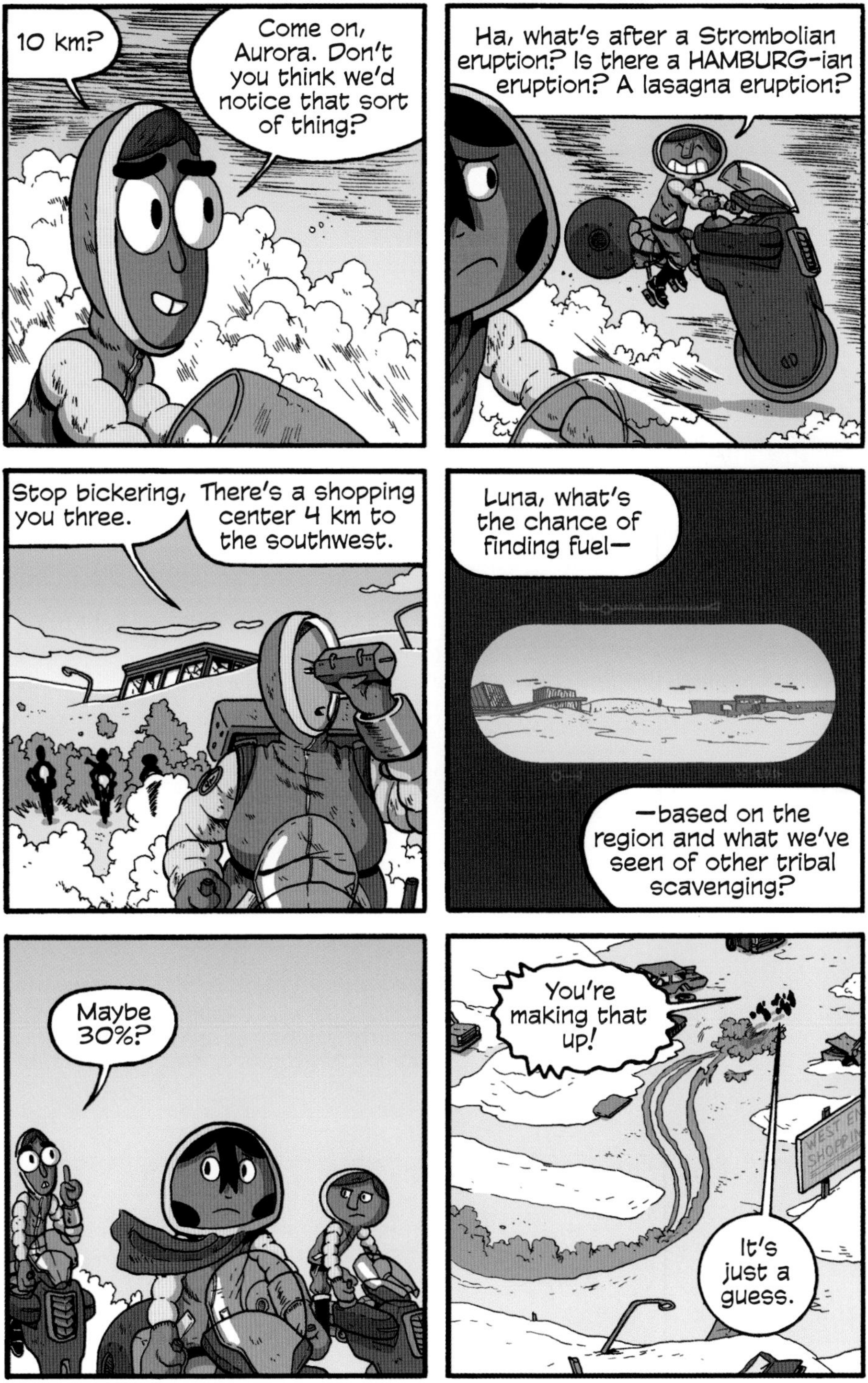
10 km?
Come on, Aurora. Don't you think we'd notice that sort of thing?
Ha, what's after a Strombolian eruption? Is there a HAMBURG-ian eruption? A lasagna eruption?
Stop bickering, you three.
There's a shopping center 4 km to the southwest.
Luna, what's the chance of finding fuel—
—based on the region and what we've seen of other tribal scavenging?
Maybe 30%?
You're making that up!
It's just a guess.

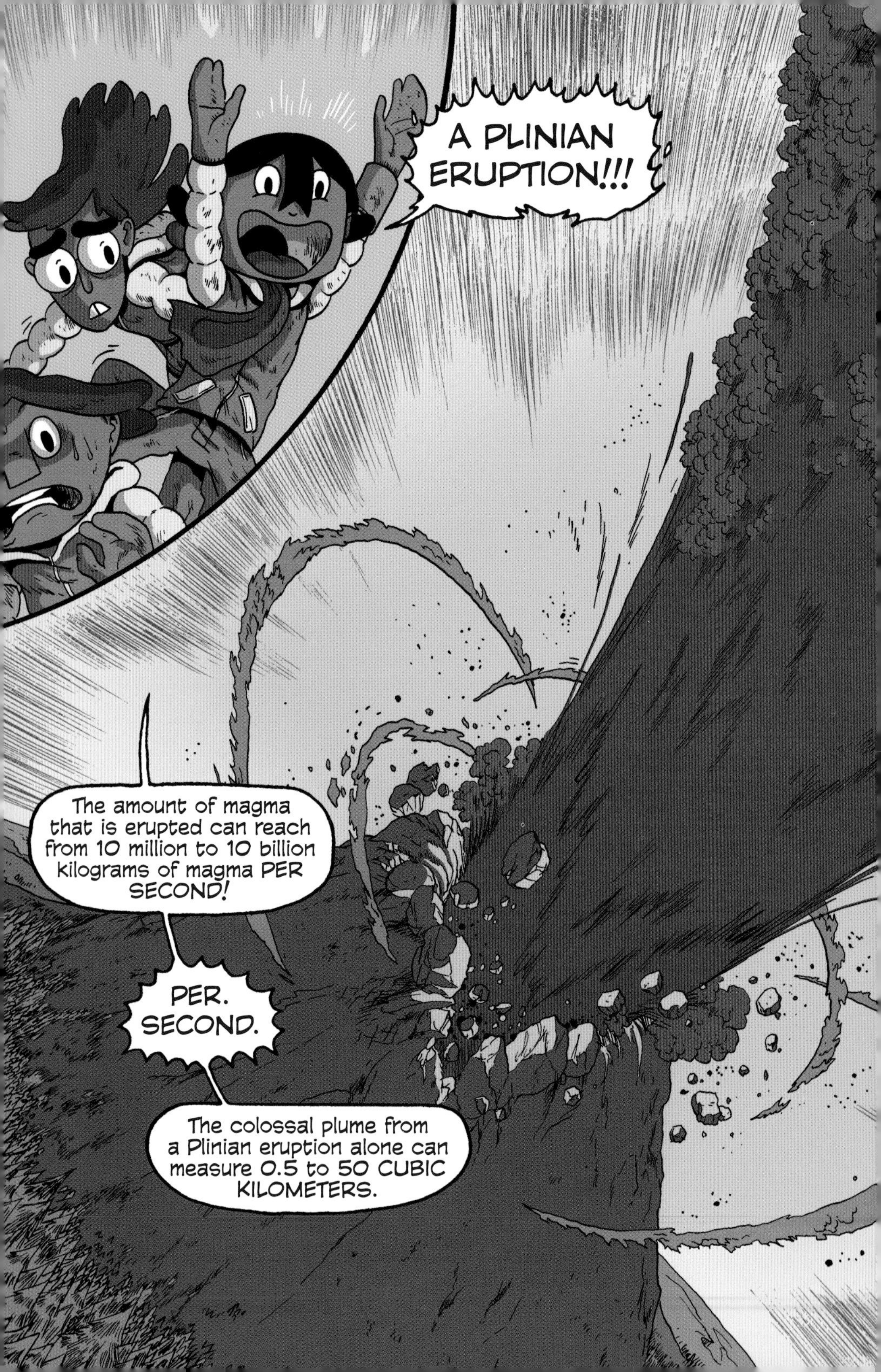
A PLINIAN ERUPTION!!!
The amount of magma that is erupted can reach from 10 million to 10 billion kilograms of magma PER SECOND!
PER. SECOND.
The colossal plume from a Plinian eruption alone can measure 0.5 to 50 CUBIC KILOMETERS.

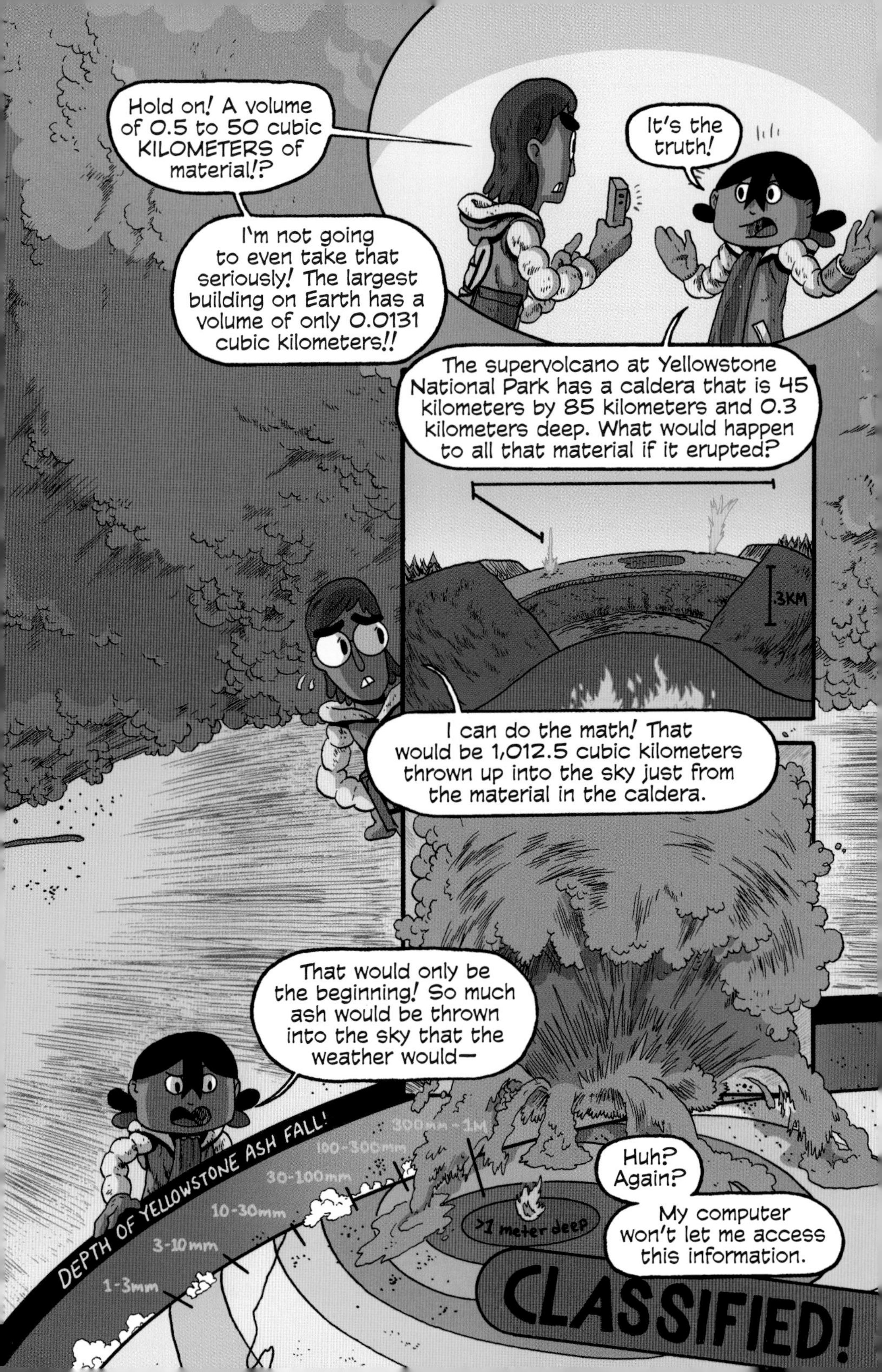
Hold on! A volume of 0.5 to 50 cubic KILOMETERS of material!?
It's the truth!
I'm not going to even take that seriously! The largest building on Earth has a volume of only 0.0131 cubic kilometers!!
The supervolcano at Yellowstone National Park has a caldera that is 45 kilometers by 85 kilometers and 0.3 kilometers deep. What would happen to all that material if it erupted?
.3KM
I can do the math! That would be 1,012.5 cubic kilometers thrown up into the sky just from the material in the caldera.
That would only be the beginning! So much ash would be thrown into the sky that the weather would—
DEPTH OF YELLOWSTONE ASH FALL!
300mm-1M
100-300mm
30-100mm
10-30mm
3-10mm
1-3mm
>1 meter deep
Huh? Again?
My computer won't let me access this information.
CLASSIFIED!

The Plinian column, or plume, is initially propelled into the sky through the sheer, pressure-packed power of the eruption.

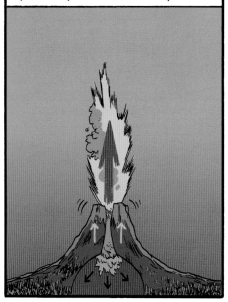

The plume is further raised by upward currents of air called CONVECTION CURRENTS.

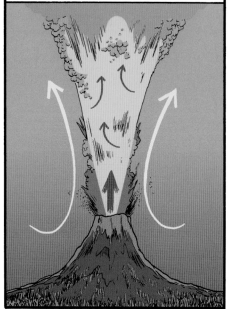

As the pressure and density of the plume balance out with that of the surrounding air, the plume levels off in what is called the "umbrella region."

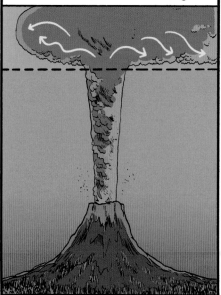

When there is not enough pressure to maintain the plume, all or part of it collapses and falls toward the ground.

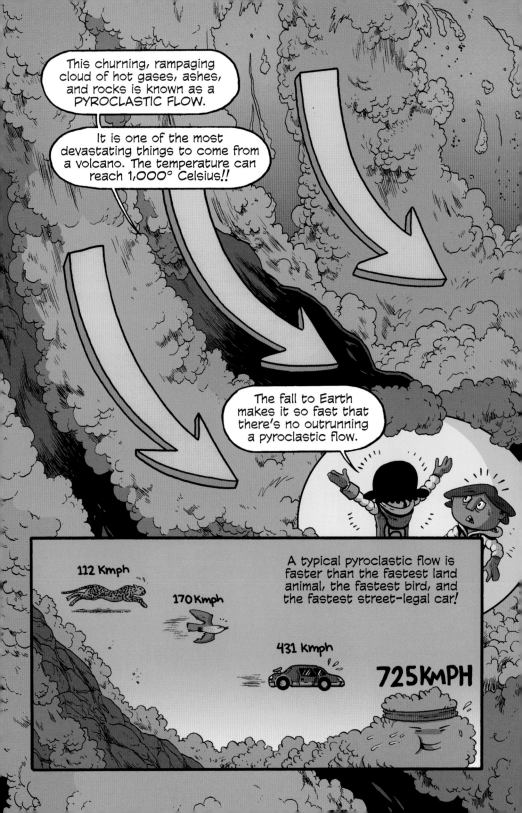

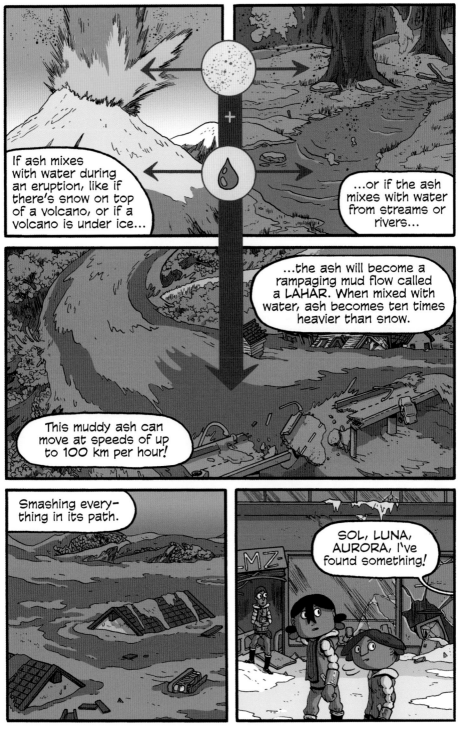

If ash mixes with water during an eruption, like if there's snow on top of a volcano, or if a volcano is under ice...

...or if the ash mixes with water from streams or rivers...

...the ash will become a rampaging mud flow called a LAHAR. When mixed with water, ash becomes ten times heavier than snow.

This muddy ash can move at speeds of up to 100 km per hour!

Smashing everything in its path.

SOL, LUNA, AURORA, I've found something!

MZ

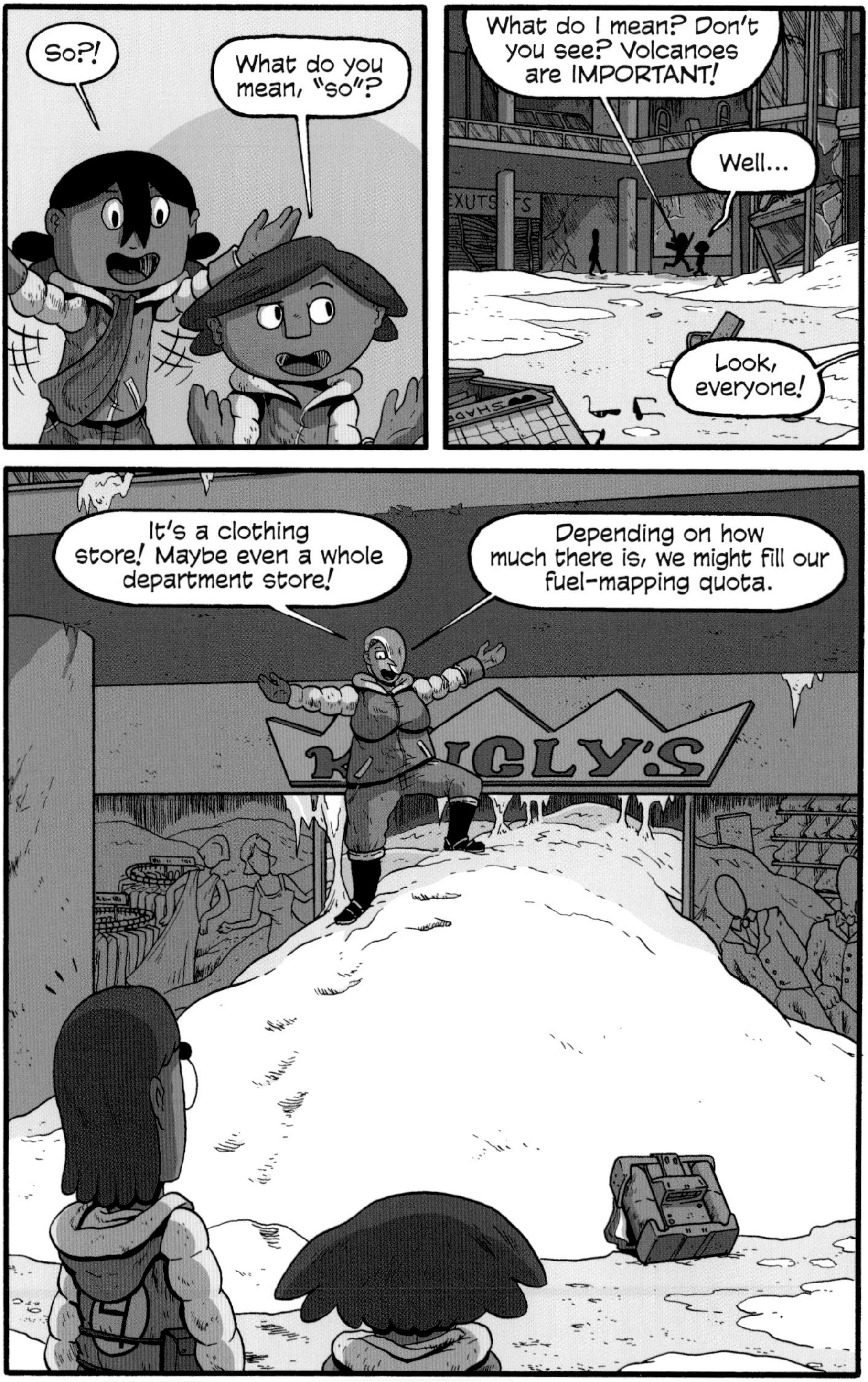
So?!
What do you mean, "so"?
What do I mean? Don't you see? Volcanoes are IMPORTANT!
Well...
EXUTS
Look, everyone!
SHADE
It's a clothing store! Maybe even a whole department store!
Depending on how much there is, we might fill our fuel-mapping quota.

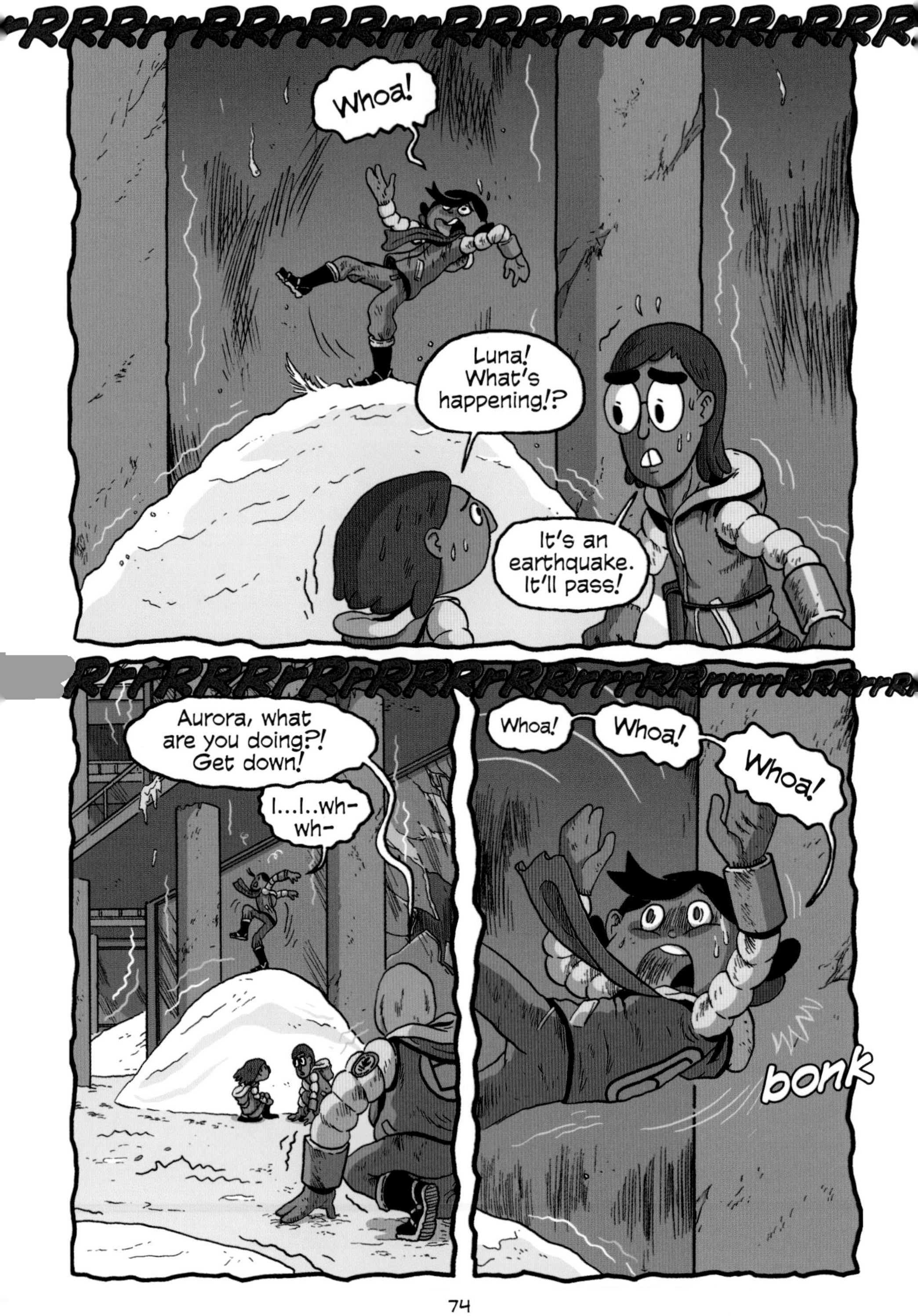
rRRRrrRRRrRRRrrRRRrRrRRRrRRR
Whoa!
Luna! What's happening!?
It's an earthquake. It'll pass!
RrrRRRRrRRrRRRRrRRRrrrRRrrrrrRRRrrR
Aurora, what are you doing?! Get down!
I...I..wh-wh-
Whoa!
Whoa!
Whoa!
bonk

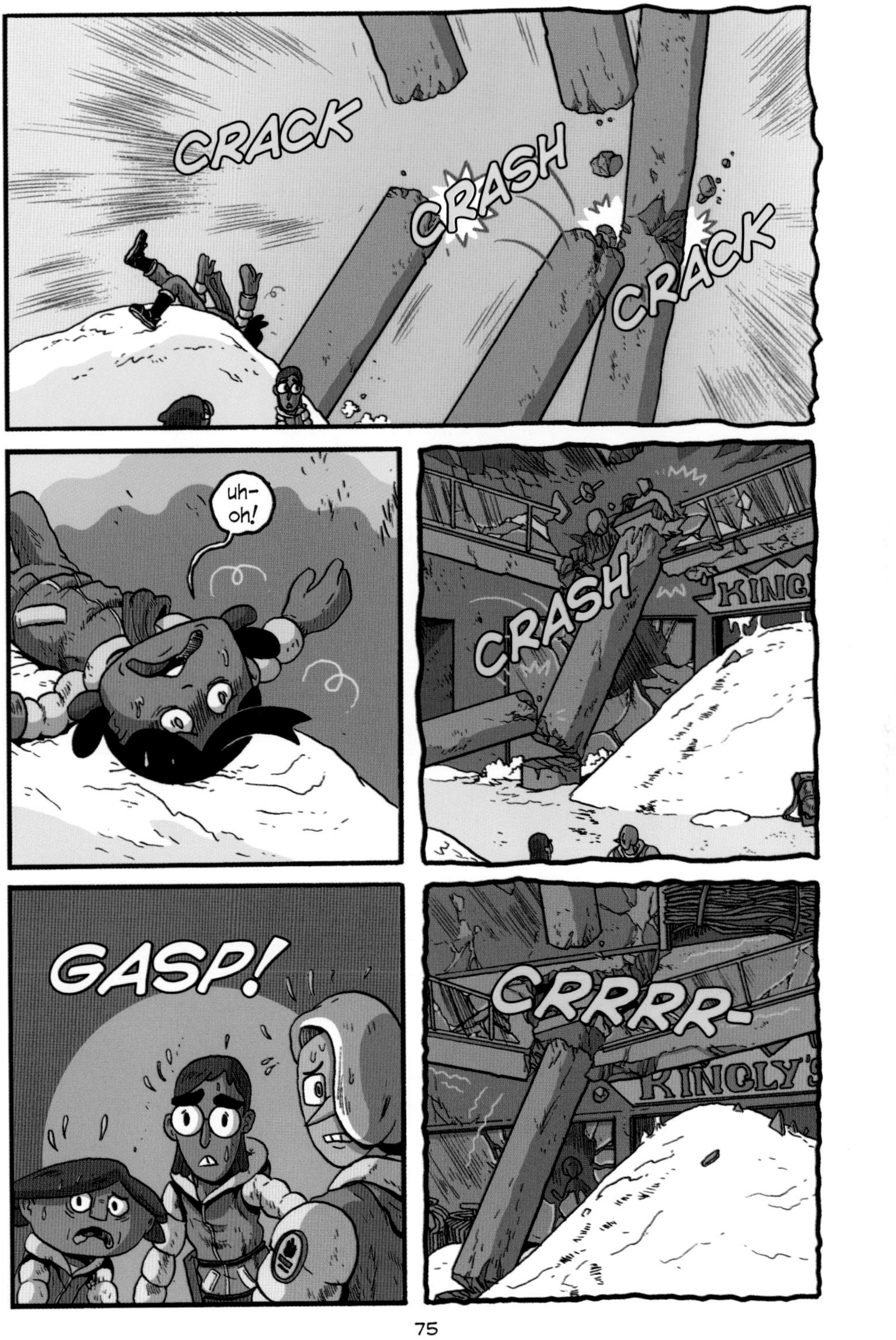
CRACK
CRASH
CRACK
uh-oh!
CRASH
KING
GASP!
CRRRR-
KINGLY'S

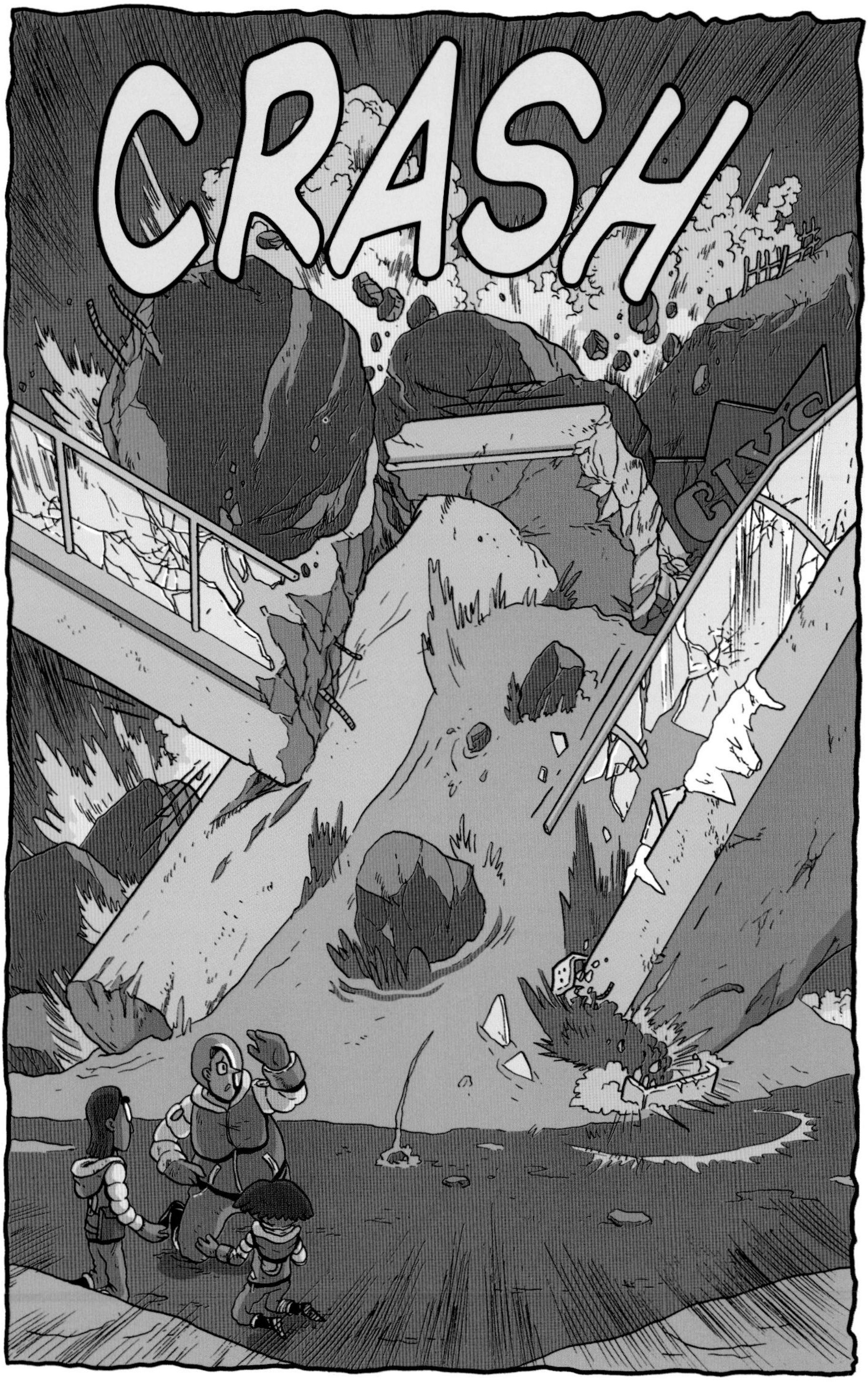
CRASH
CIVIC

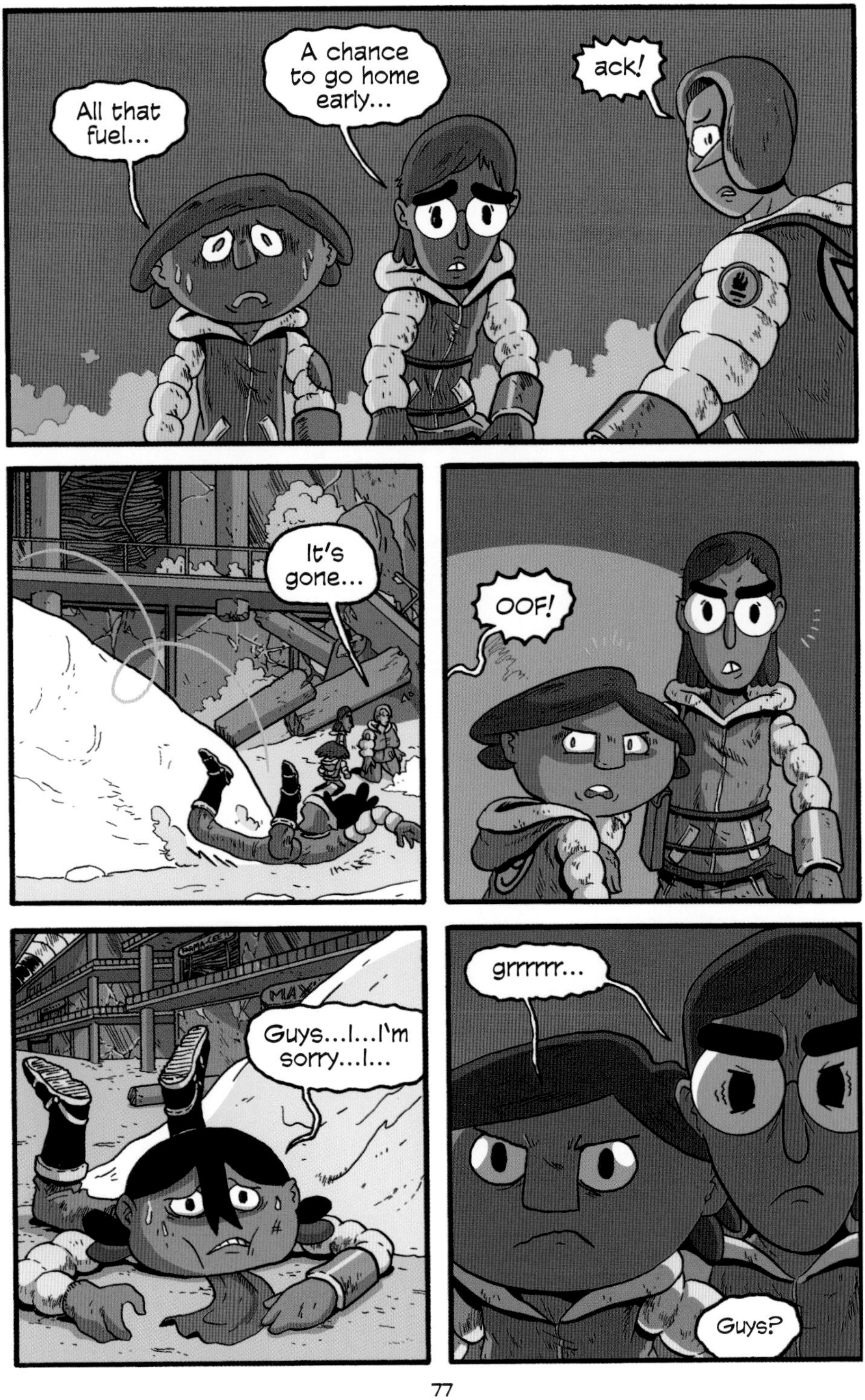
All that fuel...
A chance to go home early...
ack!
It's gone...
OOF!
Guys...I...I'm sorry...I...
grrrrrr...
Guys?

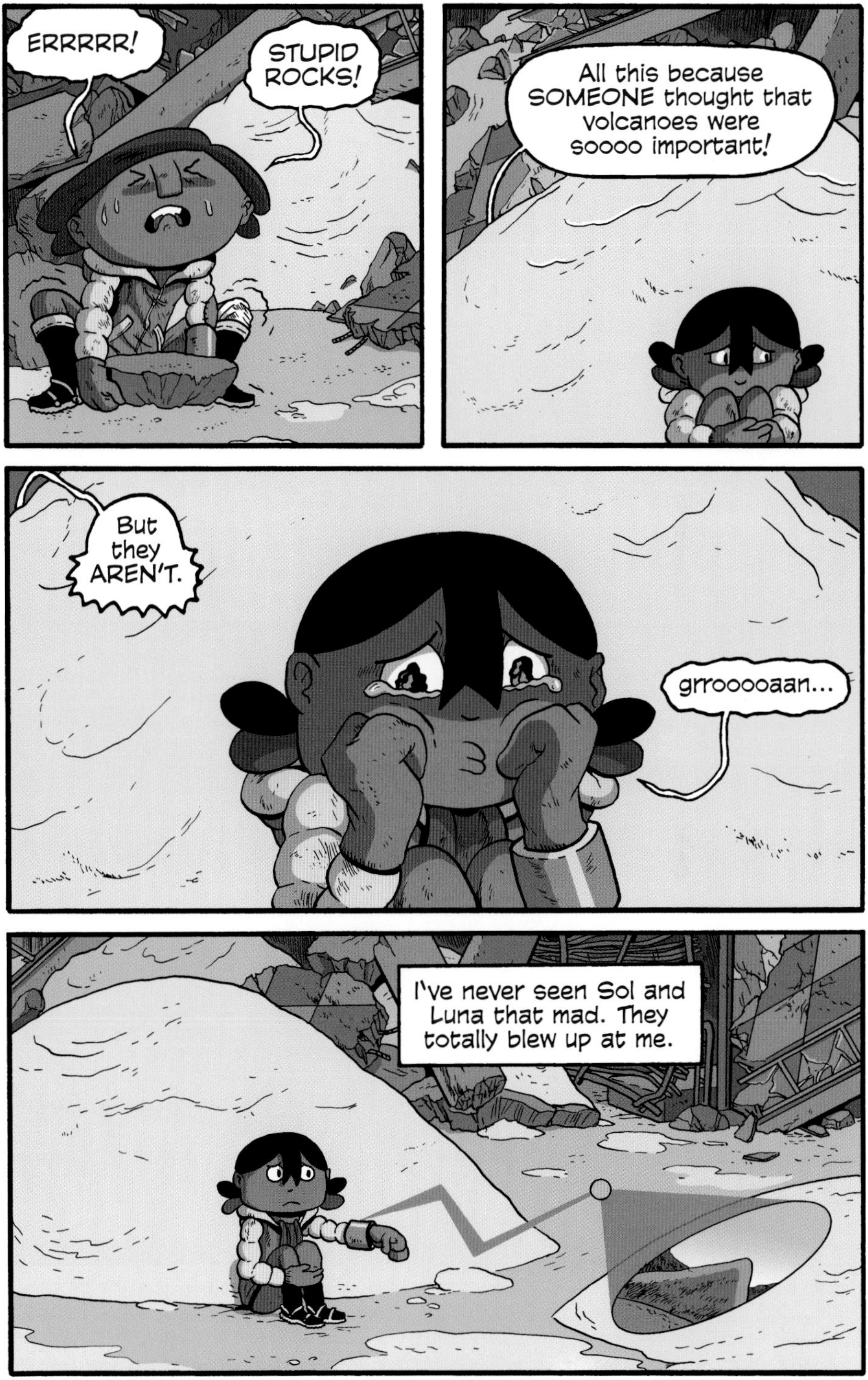
ERRRRR!
STUPID ROCKS!
All this because SOMEONE thought that volcanoes were soooo important!
But they AREN'T.
grroooooaan...
I've never seen Sol and Luna that mad. They totally blew up at me.

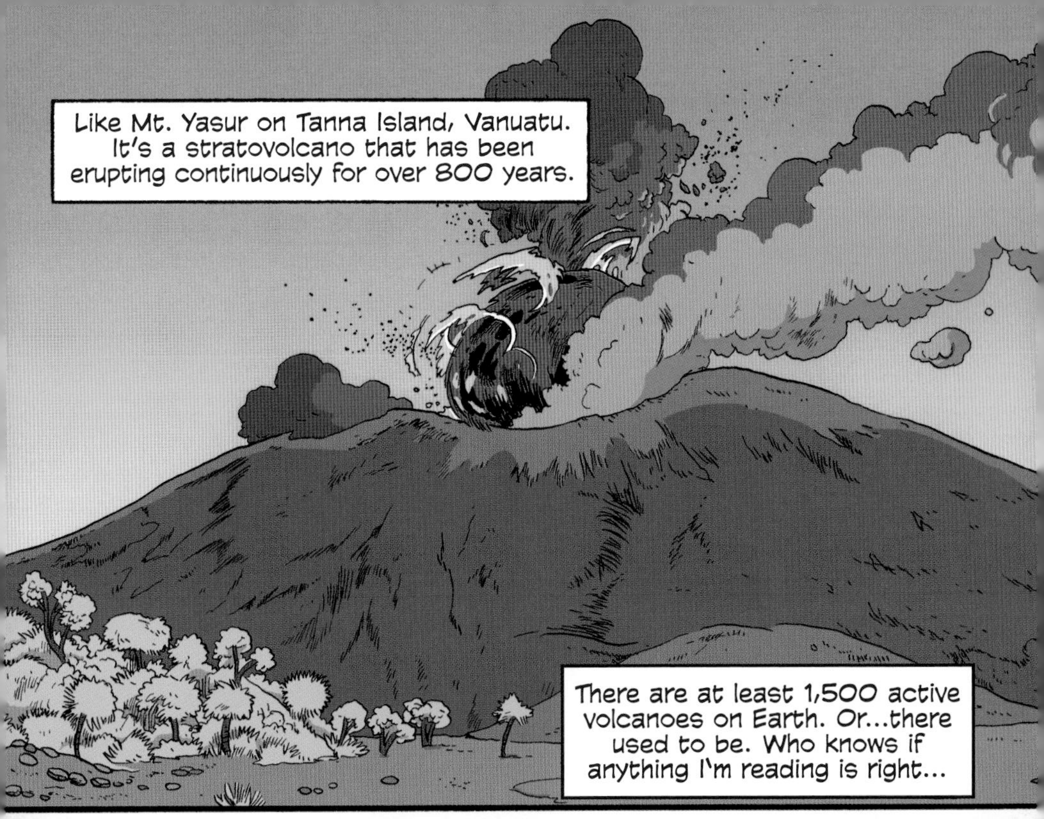
Like Mt. Yasur on Tanna Island, Vanuatu. It's a stratovolcano that has been erupting continuously for over 800 years.
There are at least 1,500 active volcanoes on Earth. Or...there used to be. Who knows if anything I'm reading is right...

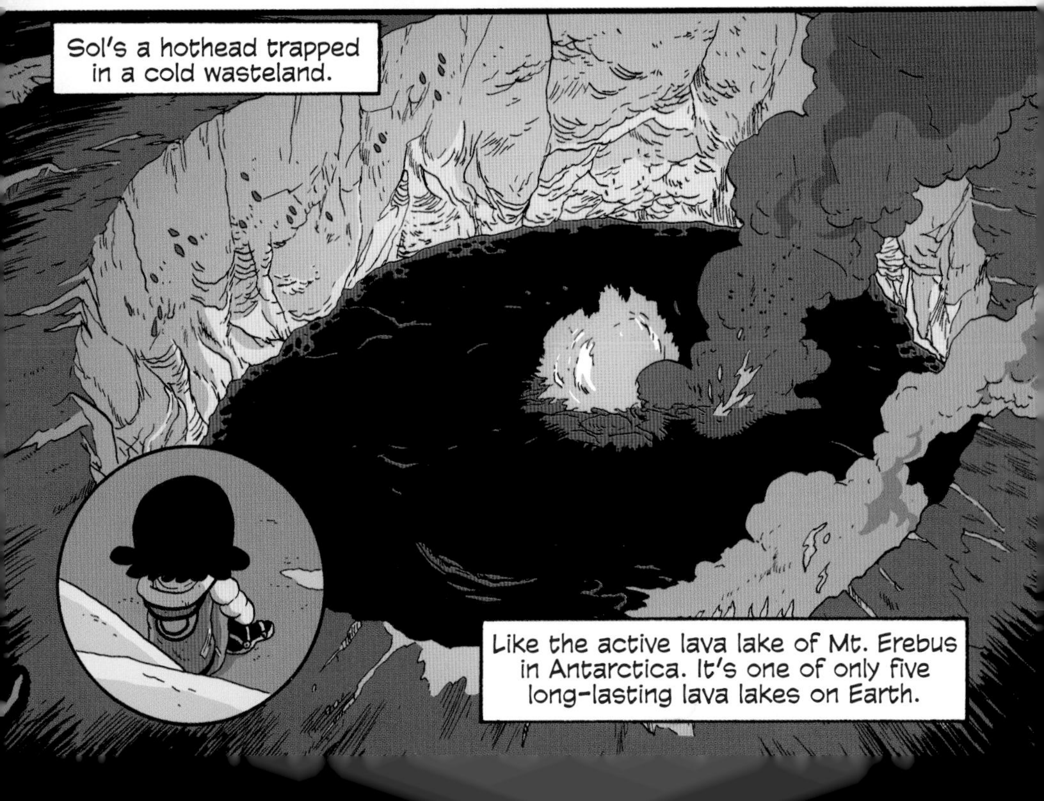
Sol's a hothead trapped in a cold wasteland.
Like the active lava lake of Mt. Erebus in Antarctica. It's one of only five long-lasting lava lakes on Earth.

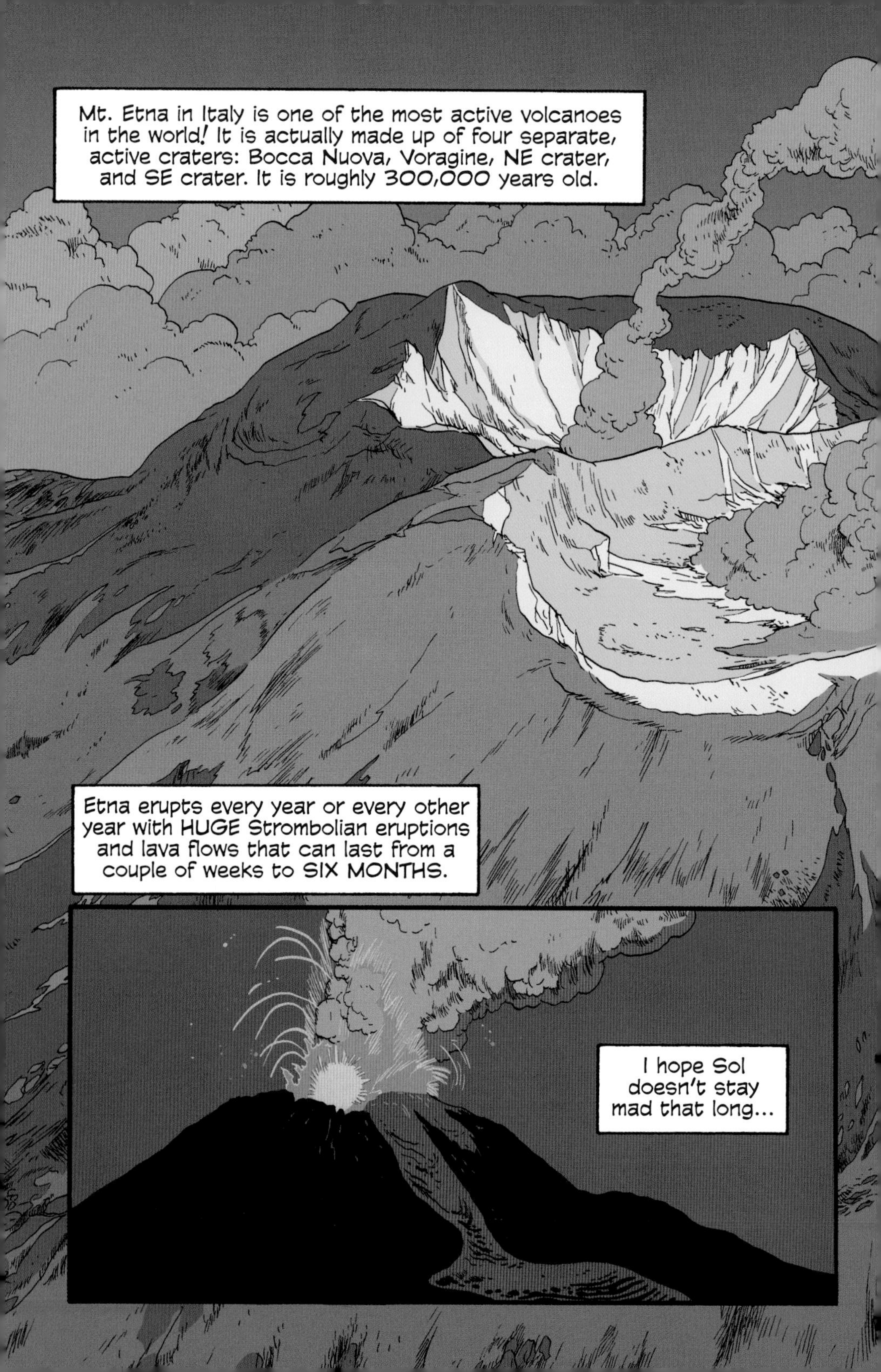
Mt. Etna in Italy is one of the most active volcanoes in the world! It is actually made up of four separate, active craters: Bocca Nuova, Voragine, NE crater, and SE crater. It is roughly 300,000 years old.
Etna erupts every year or every other year with HUGE Strombolian eruptions and lava flows that can last from a couple of weeks to SIX MONTHS.
I hope Sol doesn't stay mad that long...

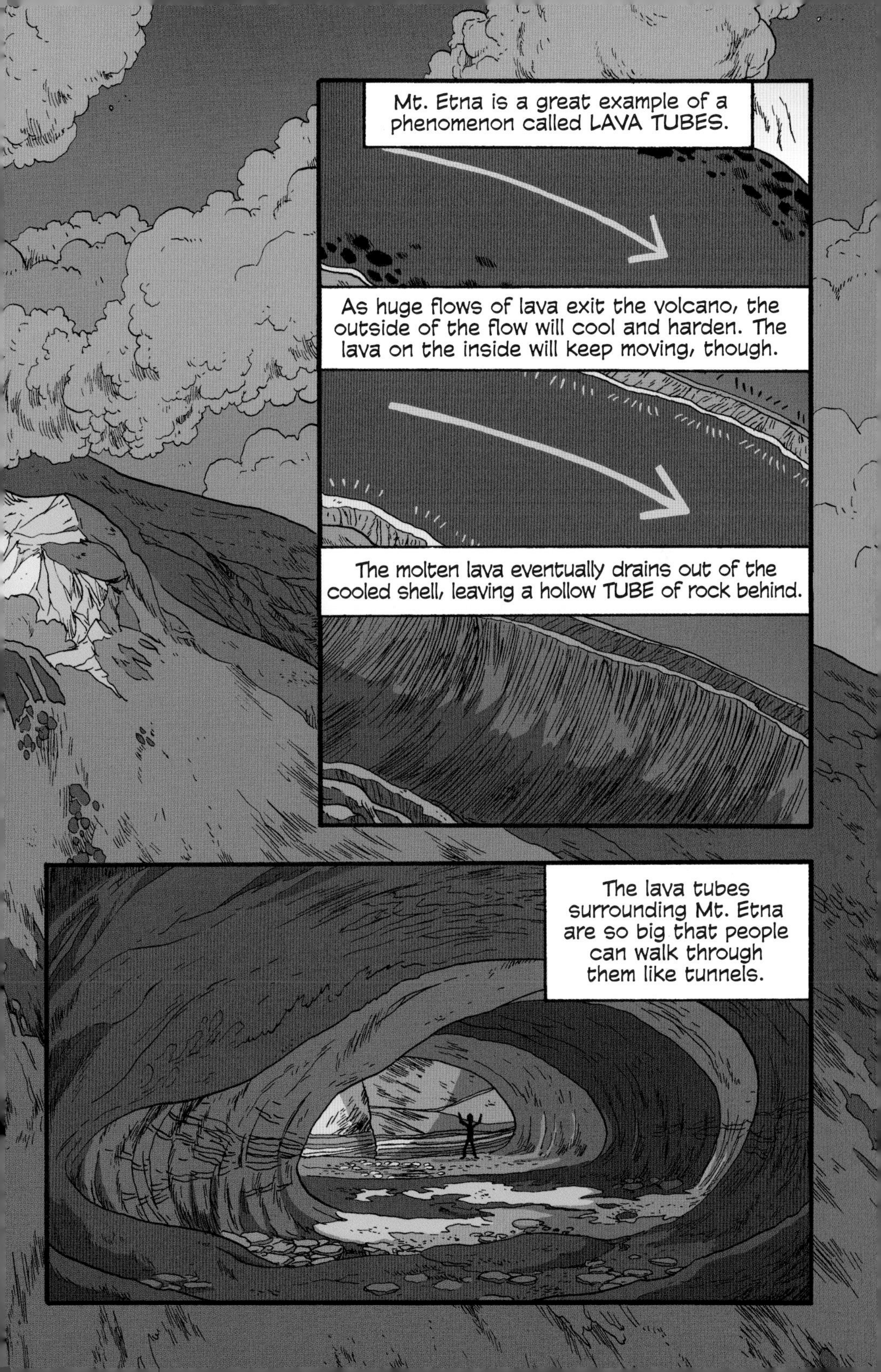

Mt. Etna is a great example of a phenomenon called LAVA TUBES.

As huge flows of lava exit the volcano, the outside of the flow will cool and harden. The lava on the inside will keep moving, though.

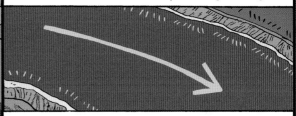

The molten lava eventually drains out of the cooled shell, leaving a hollow TUBE of rock behind.

The lava tubes surrounding Mt. Etna are so big that people can walk through them like tunnels.

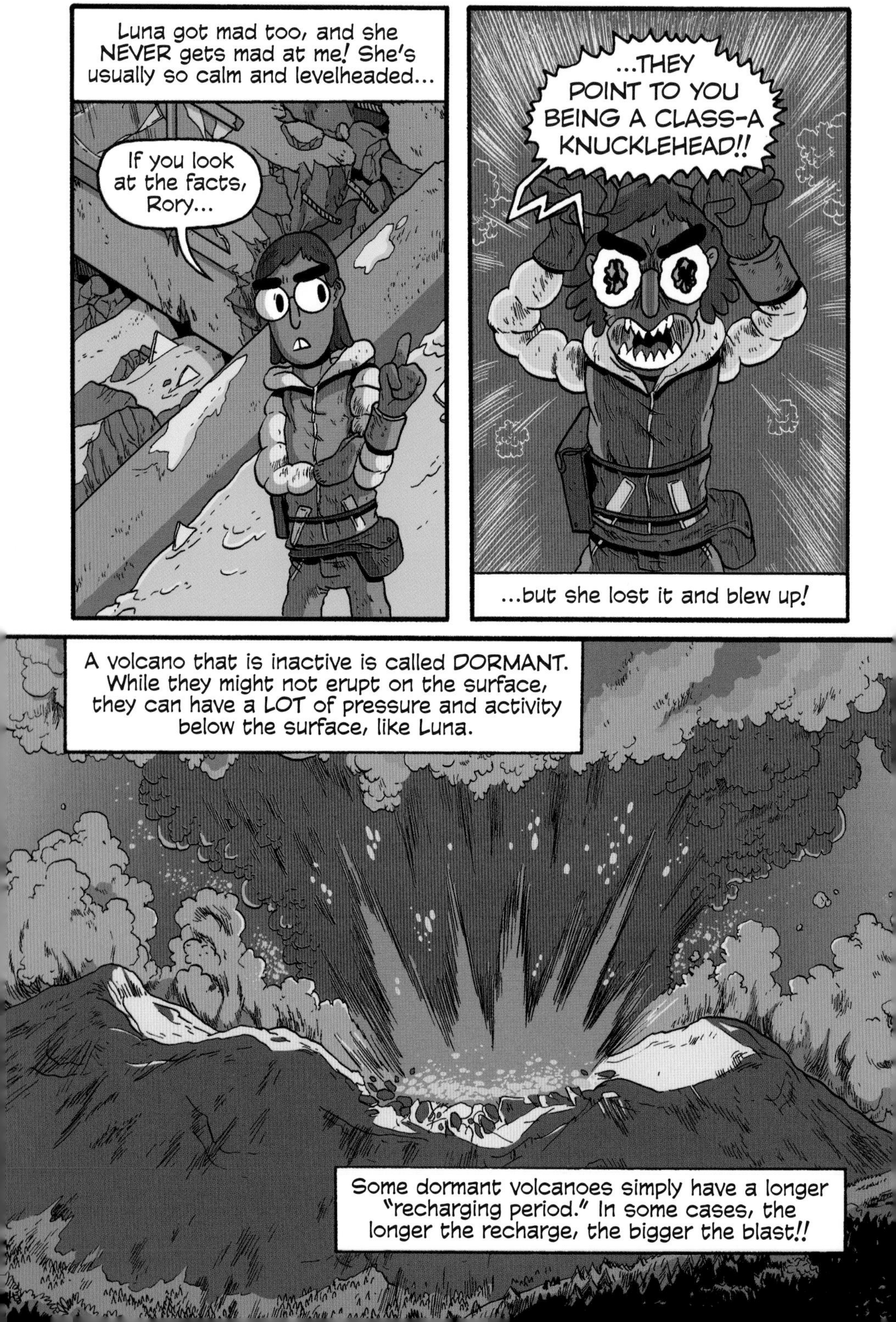
Luna got mad too, and she NEVER gets mad at me! She's usually so calm and levelheaded...
If you look at the facts, Rory...
...THEY POINT TO YOU BEING A CLASS-A KNUCKLEHEAD!!
...but she lost it and blew up!
A volcano that is inactive is called DORMANT. While they might not erupt on the surface, they can have a LOT of pressure and activity below the surface, like Luna.
Some dormant volcanoes simply have a longer "recharging period." In some cases, the longer the recharge, the bigger the blast!!

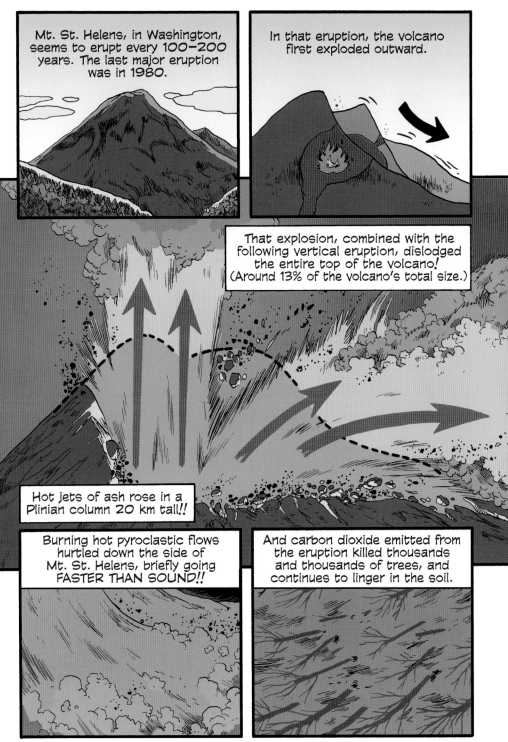

Mt. St. Helens, in Washington, seems to erupt every 100–200 years. The last major eruption was in 1980.

In that eruption, the volcano first exploded outward.

That explosion, combined with the following vertical eruption, dislodged the entire top of the volcano! (Around 13% of the volcano's total size.)

Hot jets of ash rose in a Plinian column 20 km tall!!

Burning hot pyroclastic flows hurtled down the side of Mt. St. Helens, briefly going FASTER THAN SOUND!!

And carbon dioxide emitted from the eruption killed thousands and thousands of trees, and continues to linger in the soil.

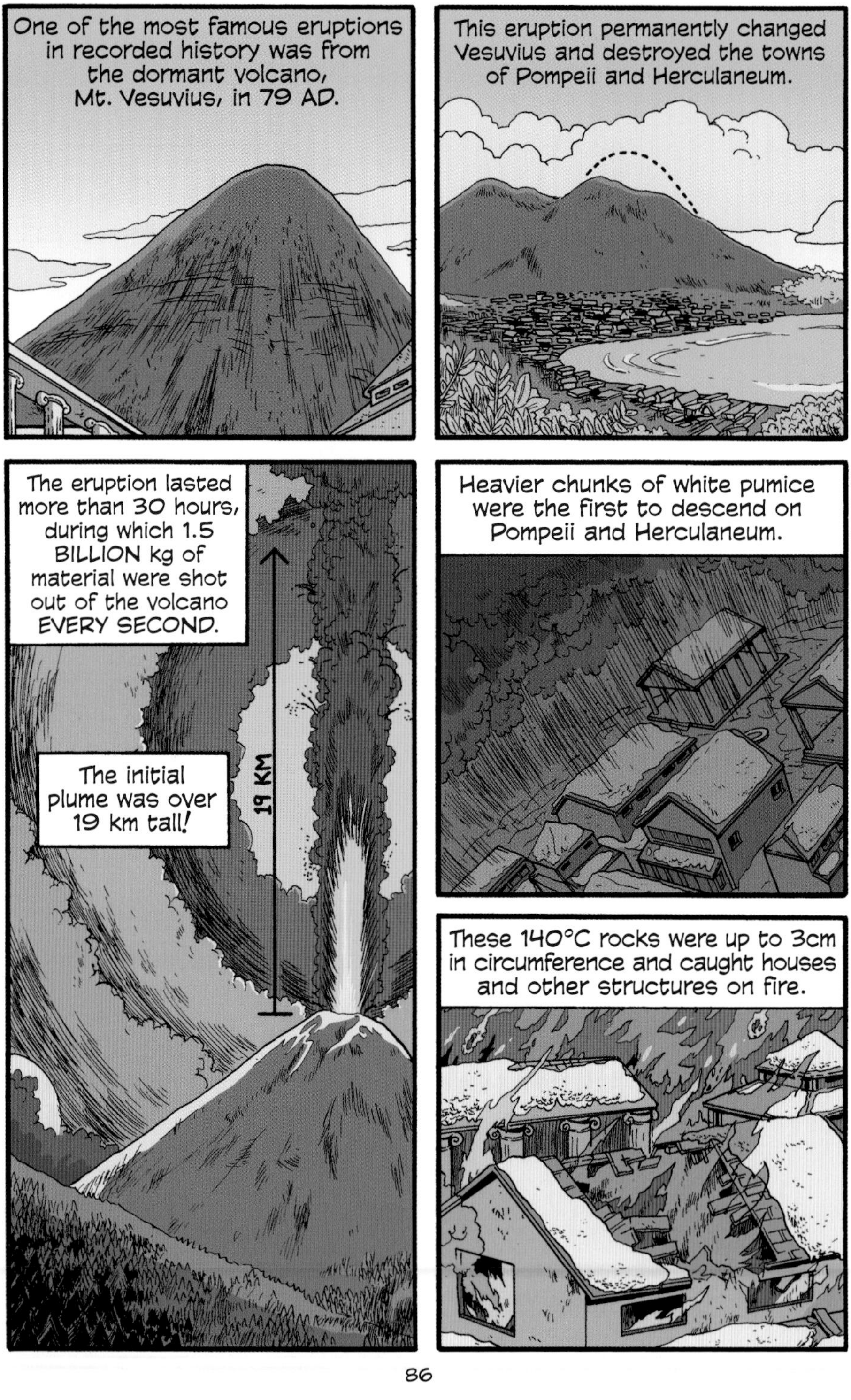
One of the most famous eruptions in recorded history was from the dormant volcano, Mt. Vesuvius, in 79 AD.
This eruption permanently changed Vesuvius and destroyed the towns of Pompeii and Herculaneum.
The eruption lasted more than 30 hours, during which 1.5 BILLION kg of material were shot out of the volcano EVERY SECOND.
19 KM
The initial plume was over 19 km tall!
Heavier chunks of white pumice were the first to descend on Pompeii and Herculaneum.
These 140°C rocks were up to 3cm in circumference and caught houses and other structures on fire.

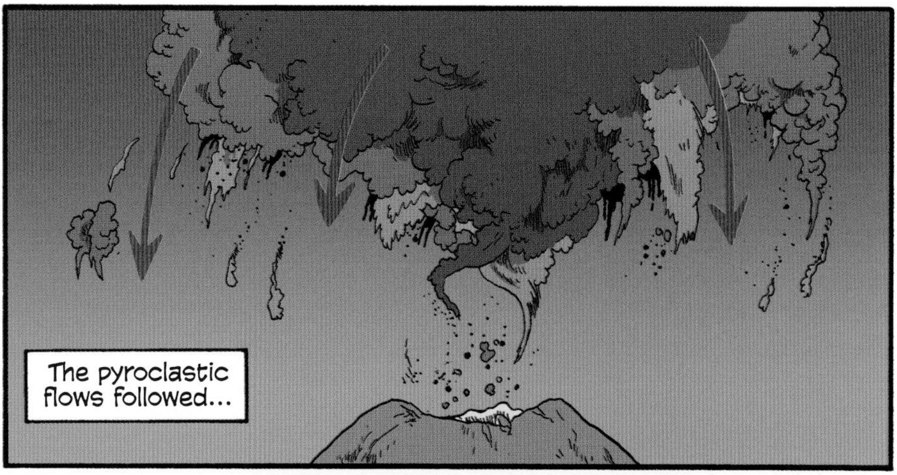
The pyroclastic flows followed...

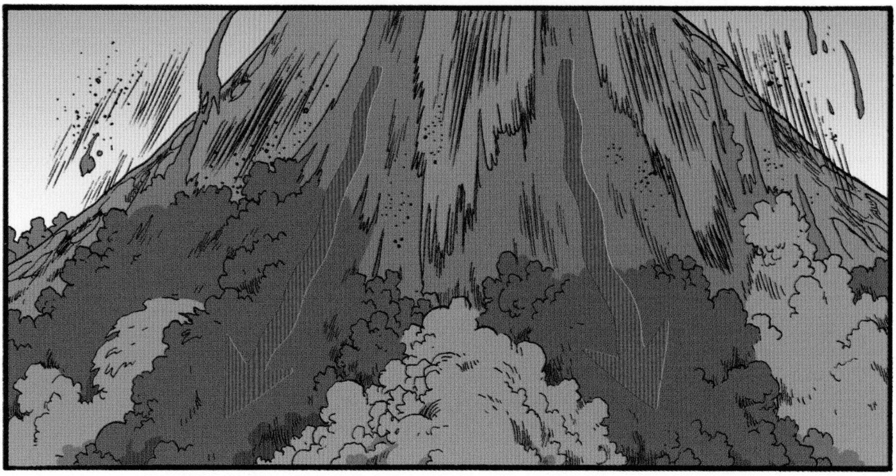

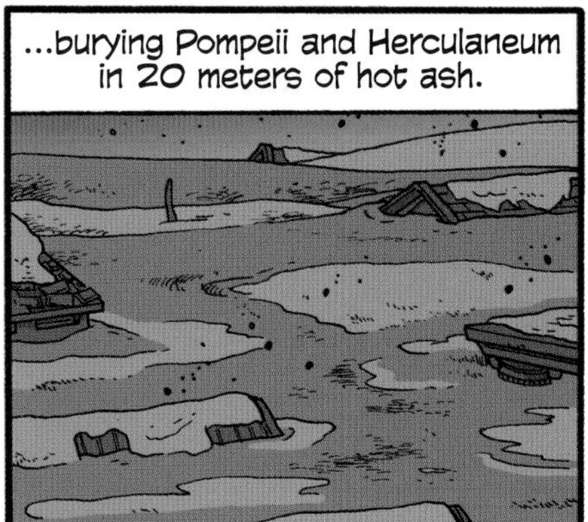
...burying Pompeii and Herculaneum in 20 meters of hot ash.

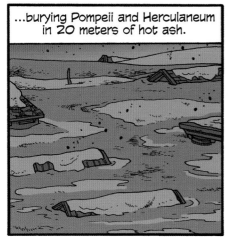

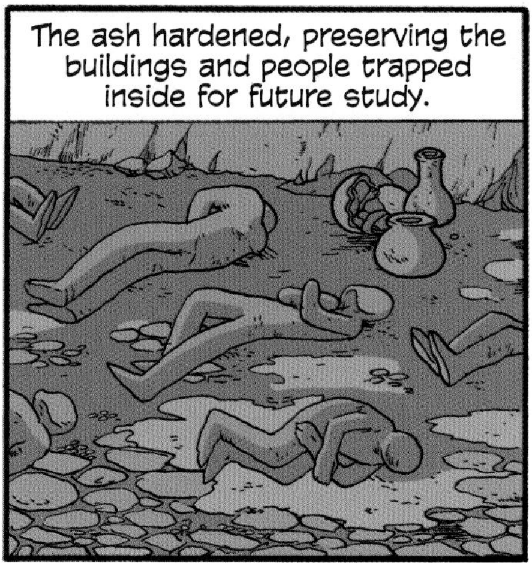
The ash hardened, preserving the buildings and people trapped inside for future study.

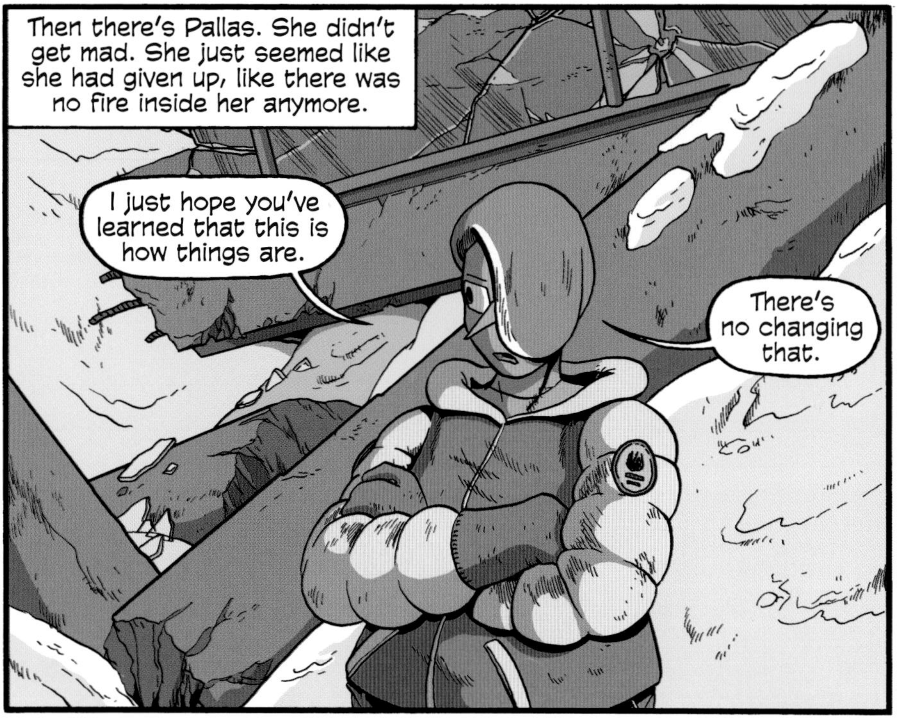
Then there's Pallas. She didn't get mad. She just seemed like she had given up, like there was no fire inside her anymore.
I just hope you've learned that this is how things are.
There's no changing that.

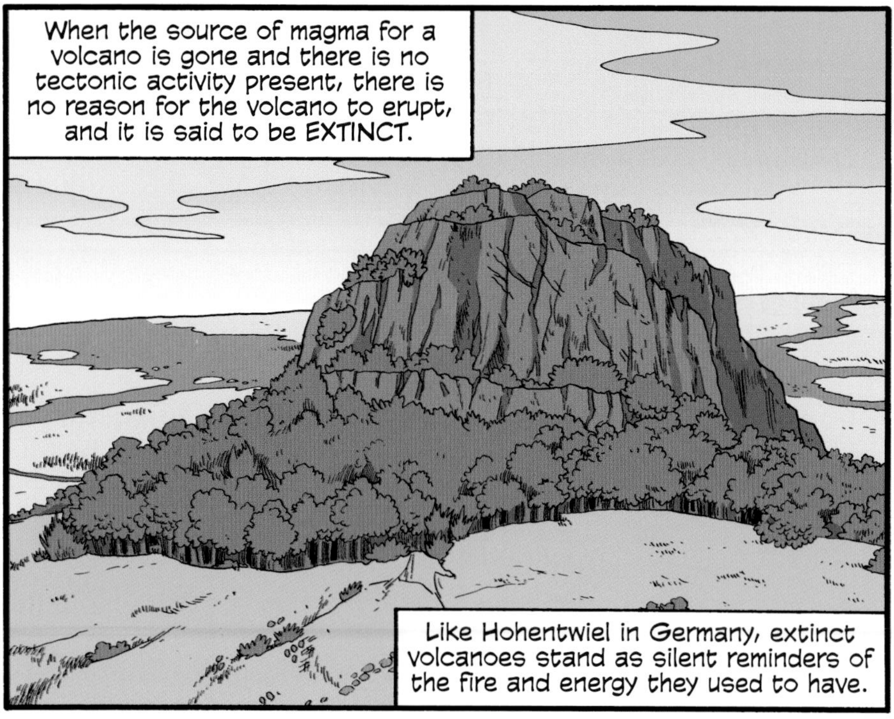
When the source of magma for a volcano is gone and there is no tectonic activity present, there is no reason for the volcano to erupt, and it is said to be EXTINCT.
Like Hohentwiel in Germany, extinct volcanoes stand as silent reminders of the fire and energy they used to have.

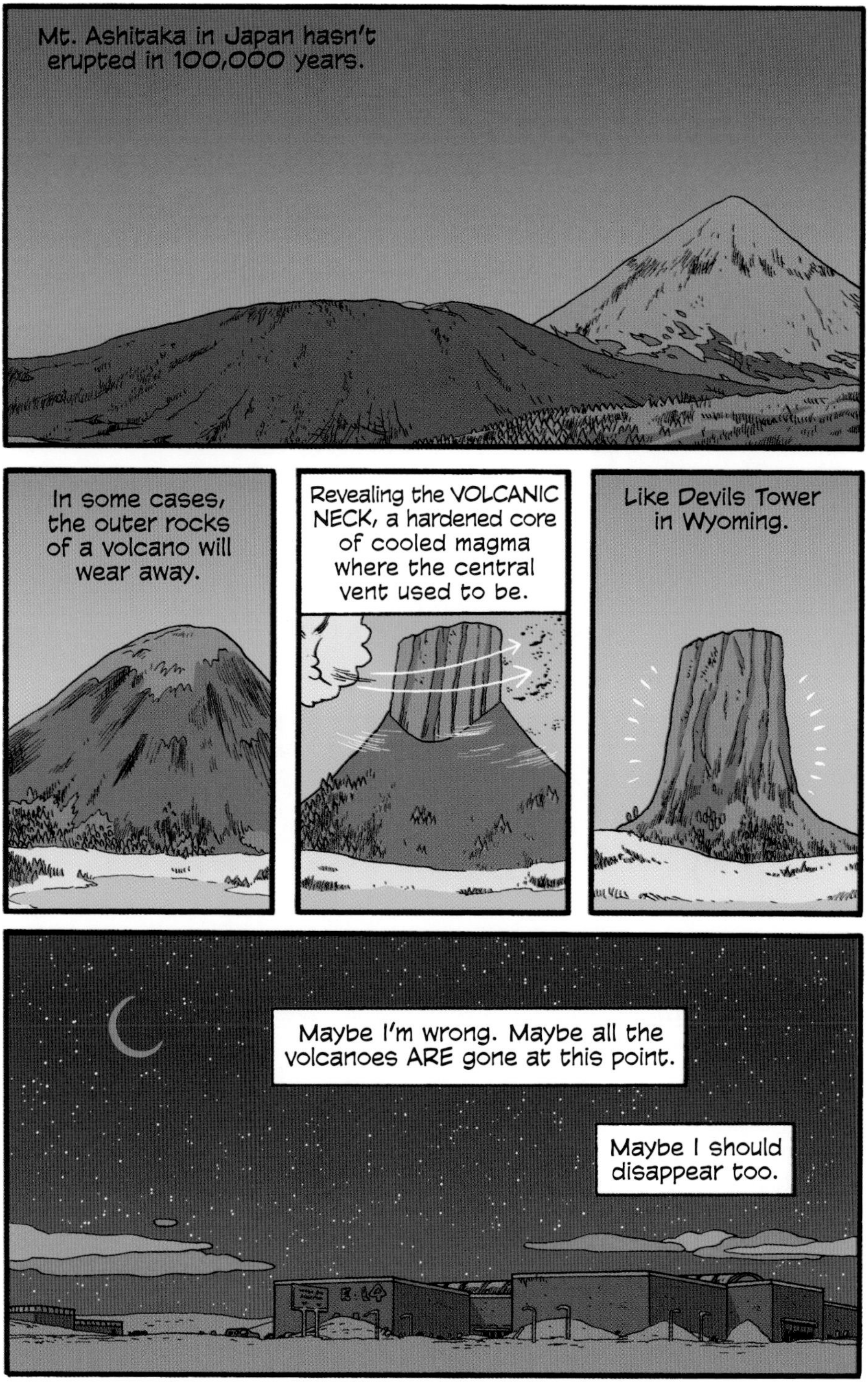
Mt. Ashitaka in Japan hasn't erupted in 100,000 years.
In some cases, the outer rocks of a volcano will wear away.
Revealing the VOLCANIC NECK, a hardened core of cooled magma where the central vent used to be.
Like Devils Tower in Wyoming.
Maybe I'm wrong. Maybe all the volcanoes ARE gone at this point.
Maybe I should disappear too.

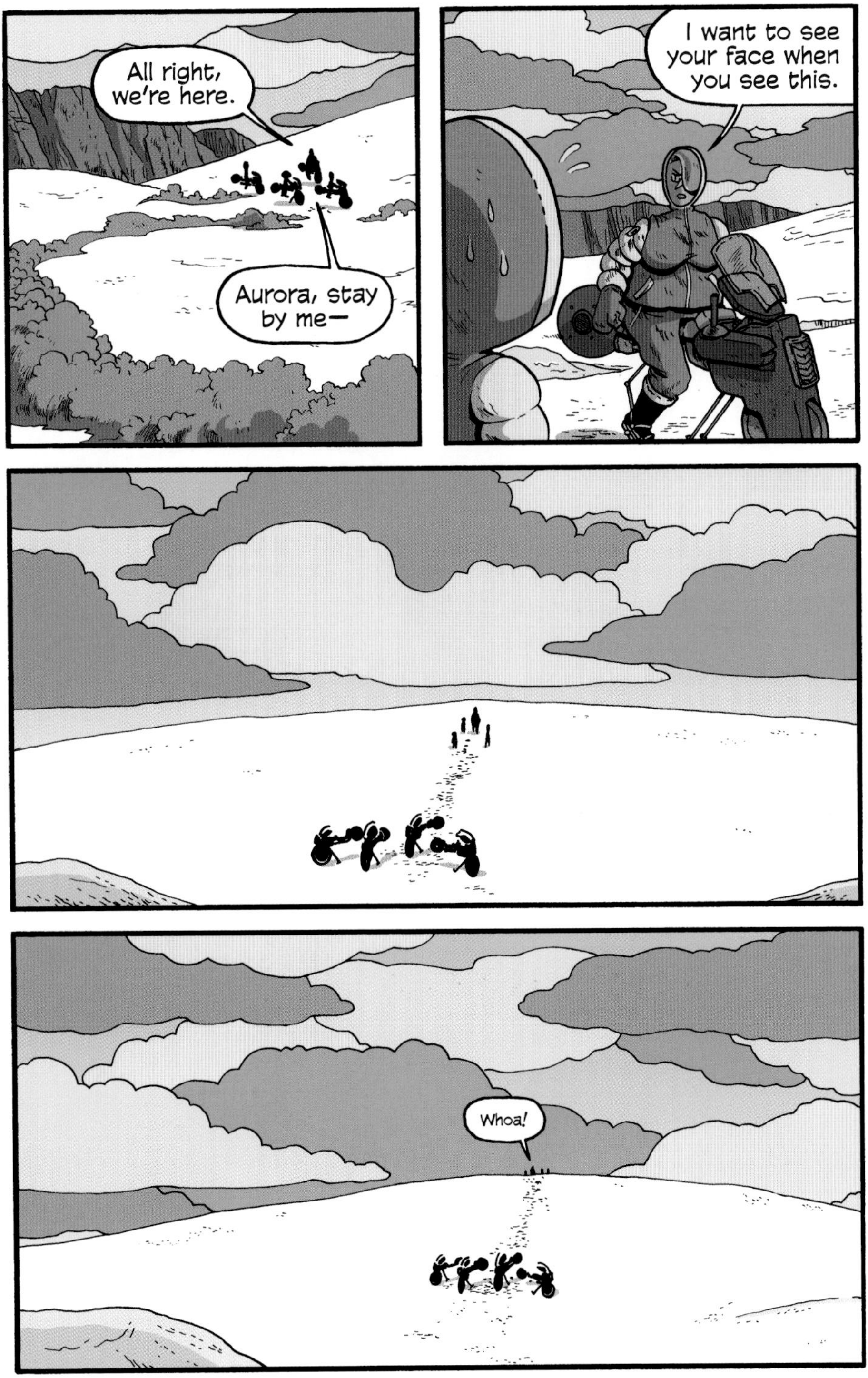
All right, we're here.
Aurora, stay by me—
I want to see your face when you see this.
Whoa!

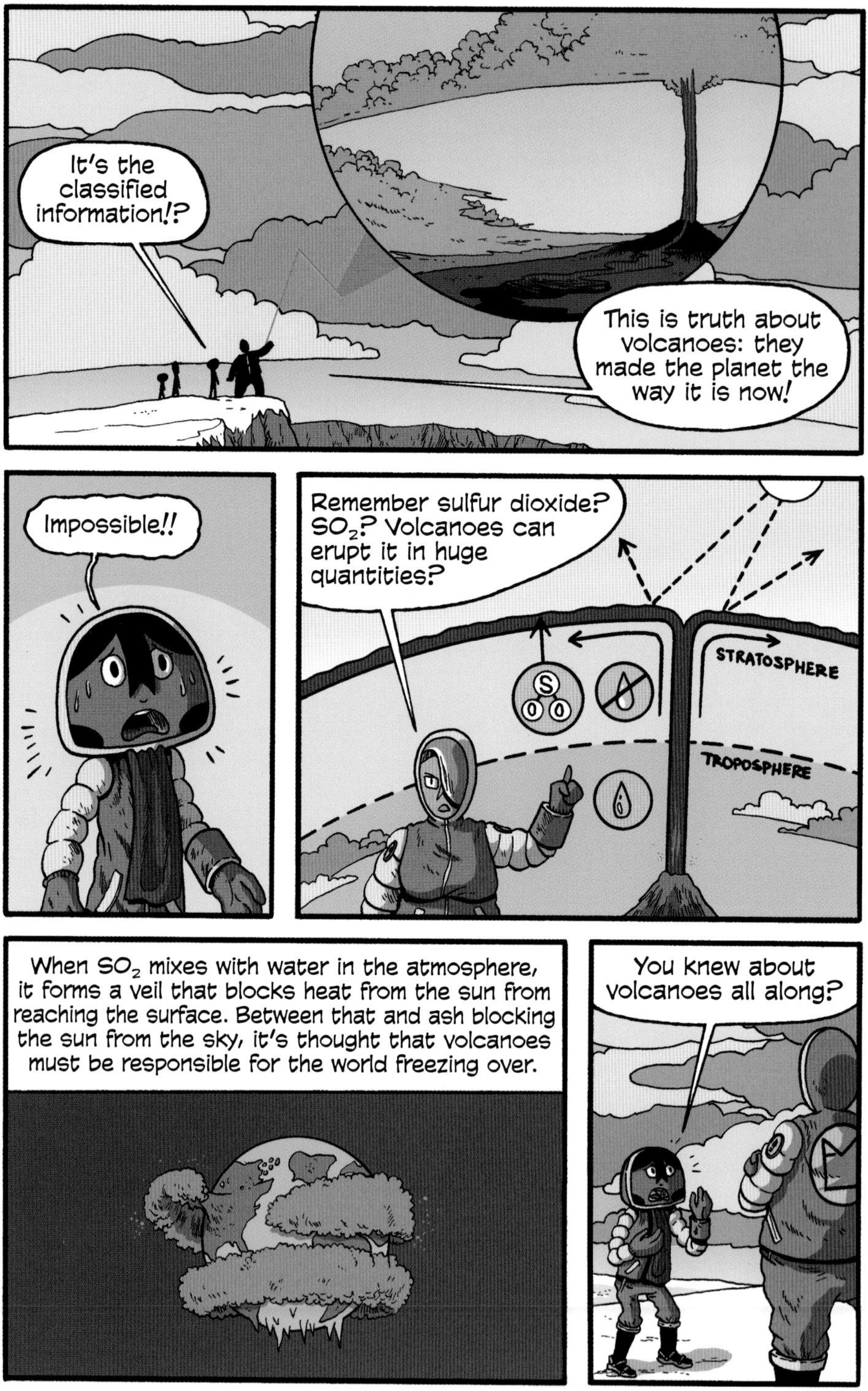

It's the classified information!?
This is truth about volcanoes: they made the planet the way it is now!
Impossible!!
Remember sulfur dioxide? SO_2? Volcanoes can erupt it in huge quantities?
STRATOSPHERE
TROPOSPHERE
S
O O
When SO_2 mixes with water in the atmosphere, it forms a veil that blocks heat from the sun from reaching the surface. Between that and ash blocking the sun from the sky, it's thought that volcanoes must be responsible for the world freezing over.
You knew about volcanoes all along?

95

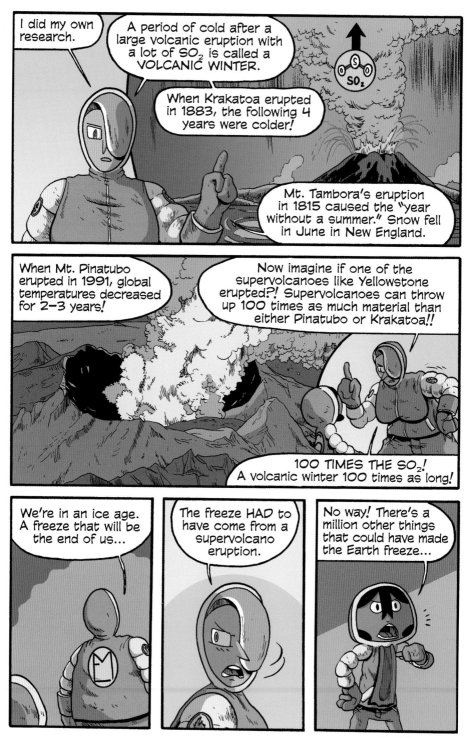

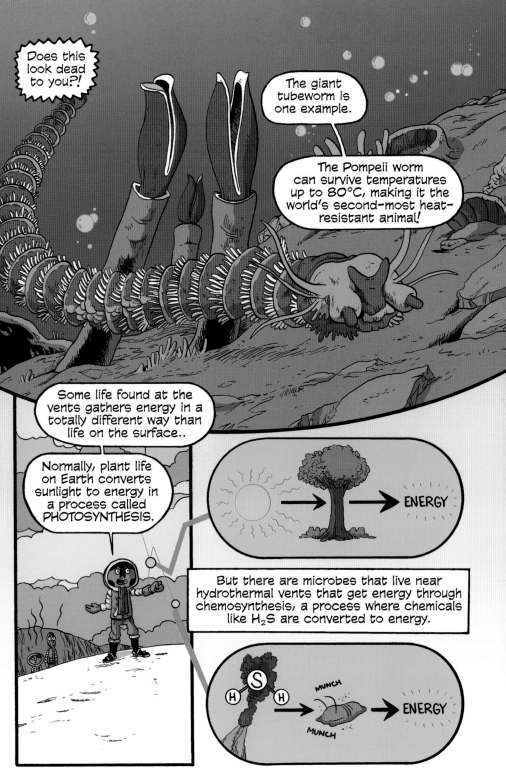

99

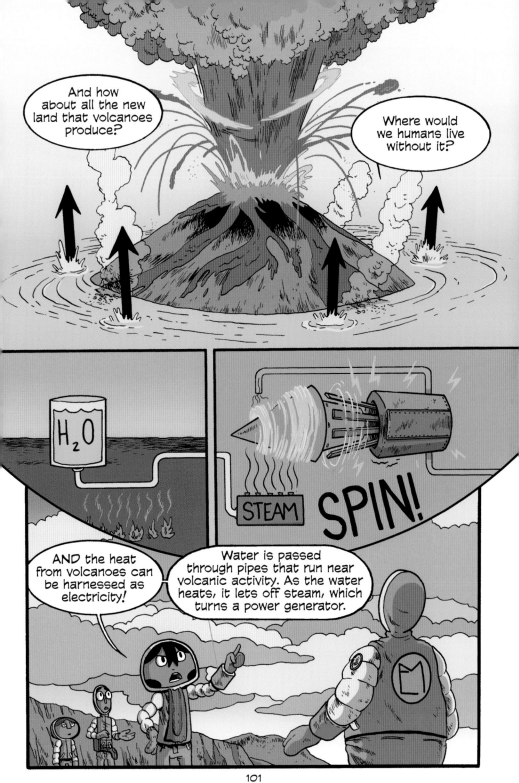

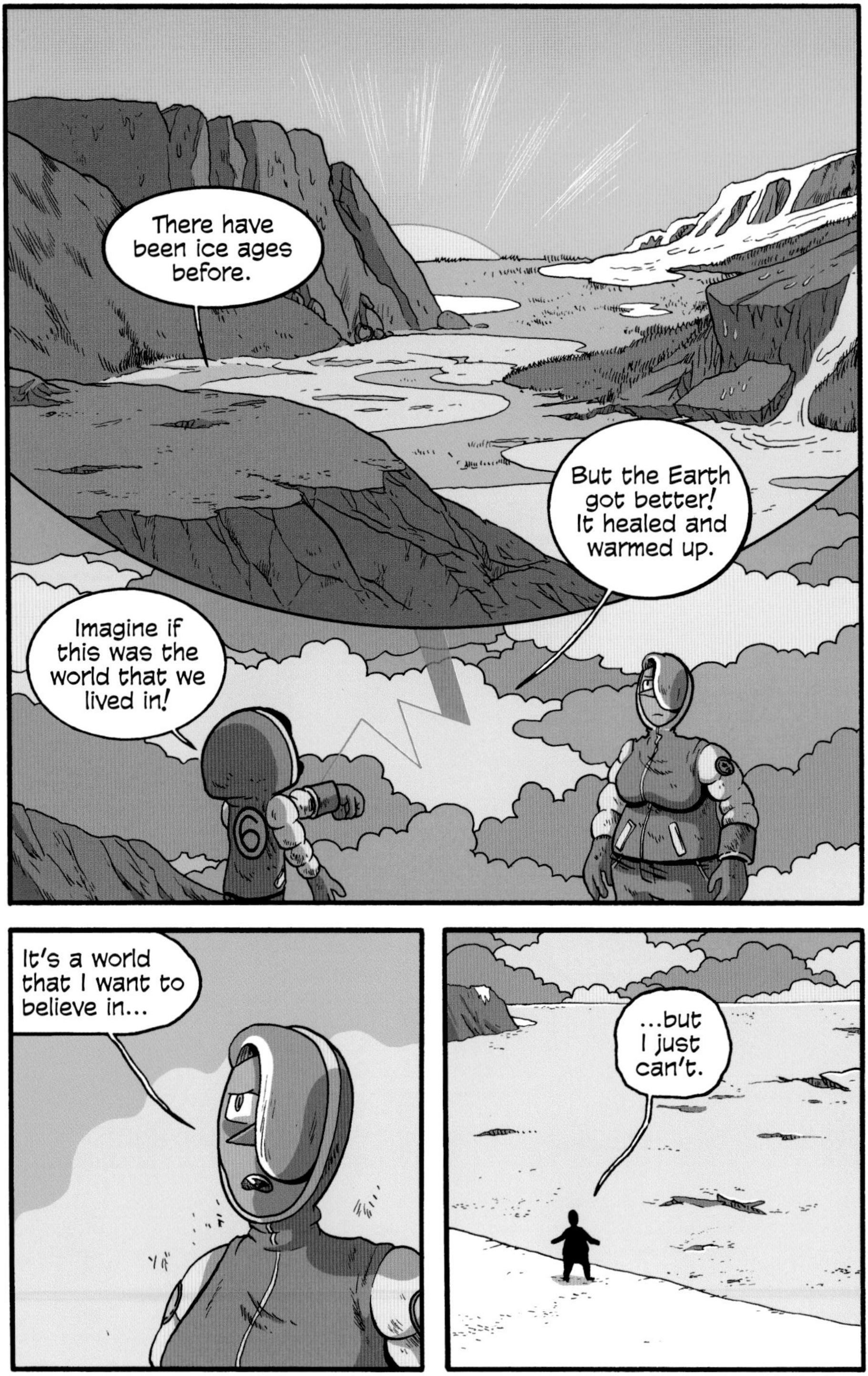
There have been ice ages before.
But the Earth got better! It healed and warmed up.
Imagine if this was the world that we lived in!
It's a world that I want to believe in...
...but I just can't.

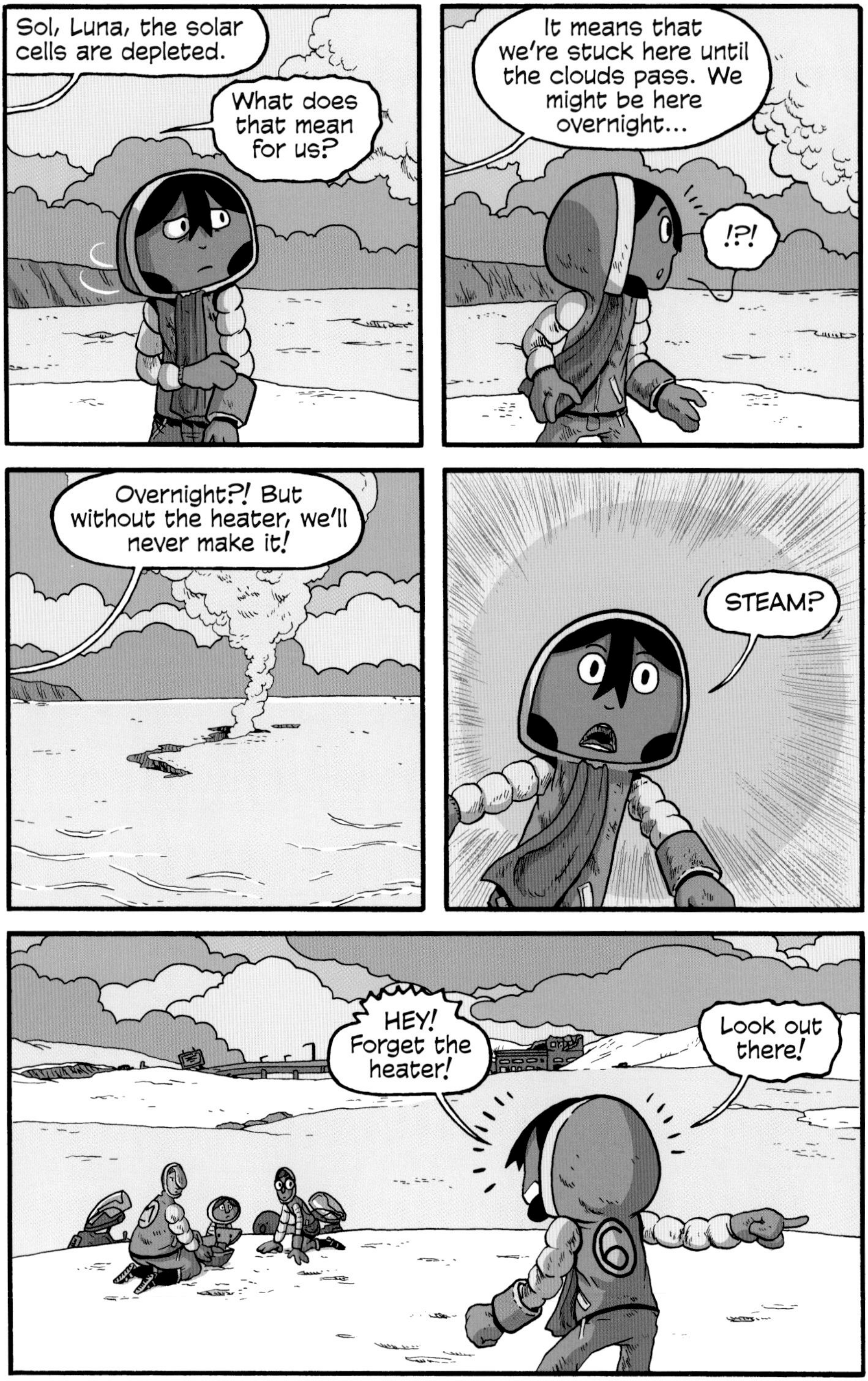
Sol, Luna, the solar cells are depleted.
What does that mean for us?
It means that we're stuck here until the clouds pass. We might be here overnight...
!?!
Overnight?! But without the heater, we'll never make it!
STEAM?
HEY! Forget the heater!
Look out there!

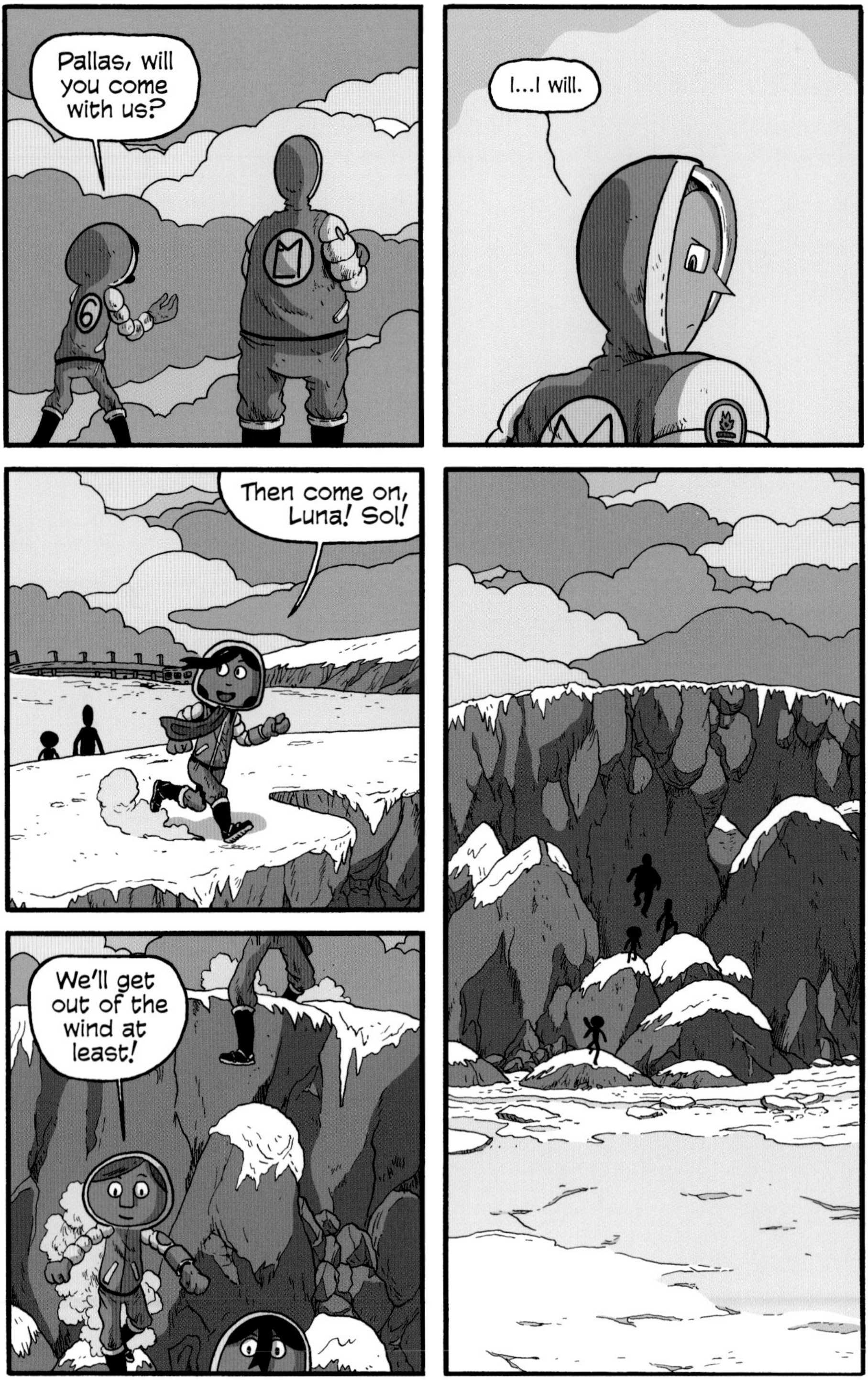
Pallas, will you come with us?
I...I will.
Then come on, Luna! Sol!
We'll get out of the wind at least!

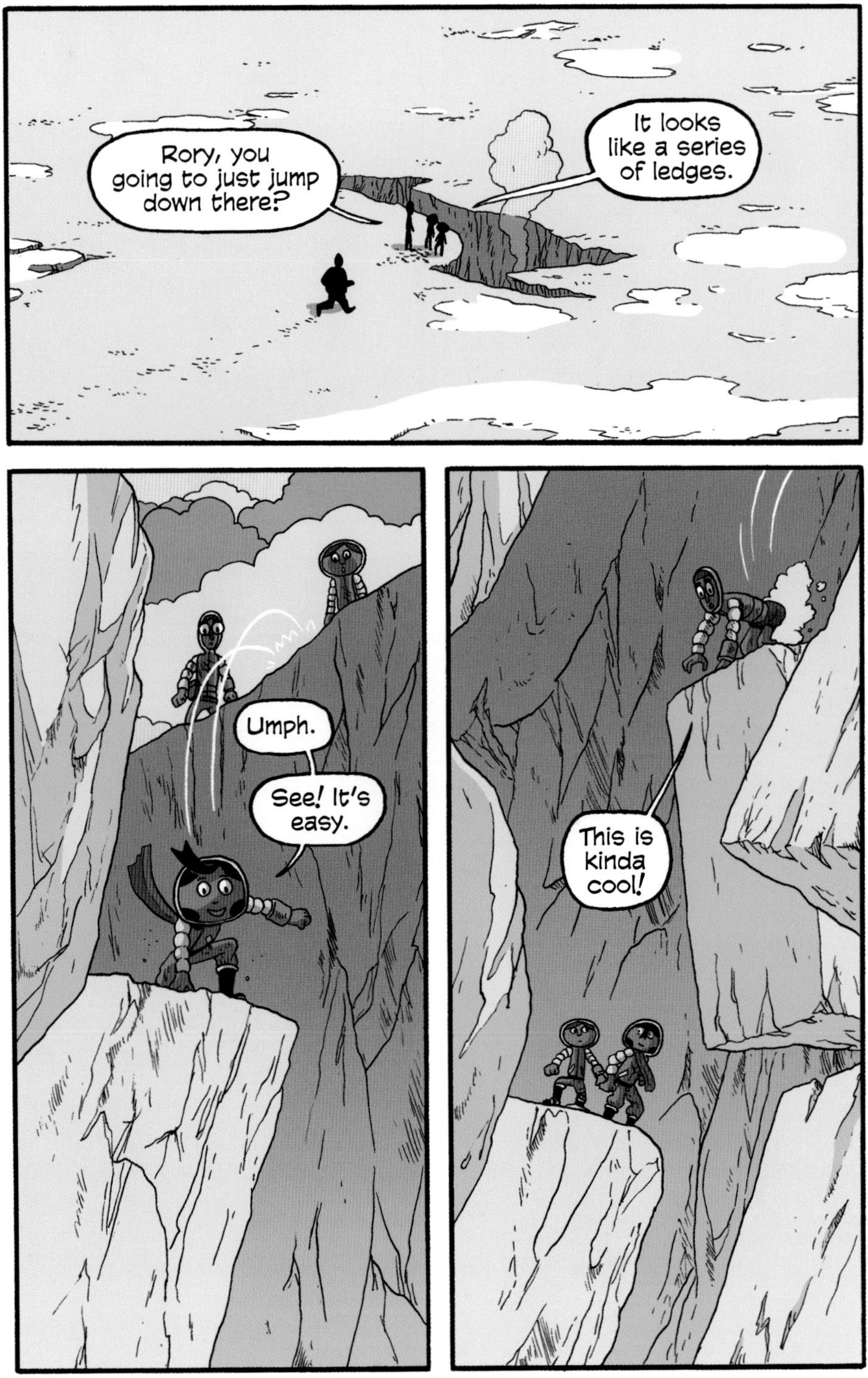
Rory, you going to just jump down there?
It looks like a series of ledges.
Umph.
See! It's easy.
This is kinda cool!

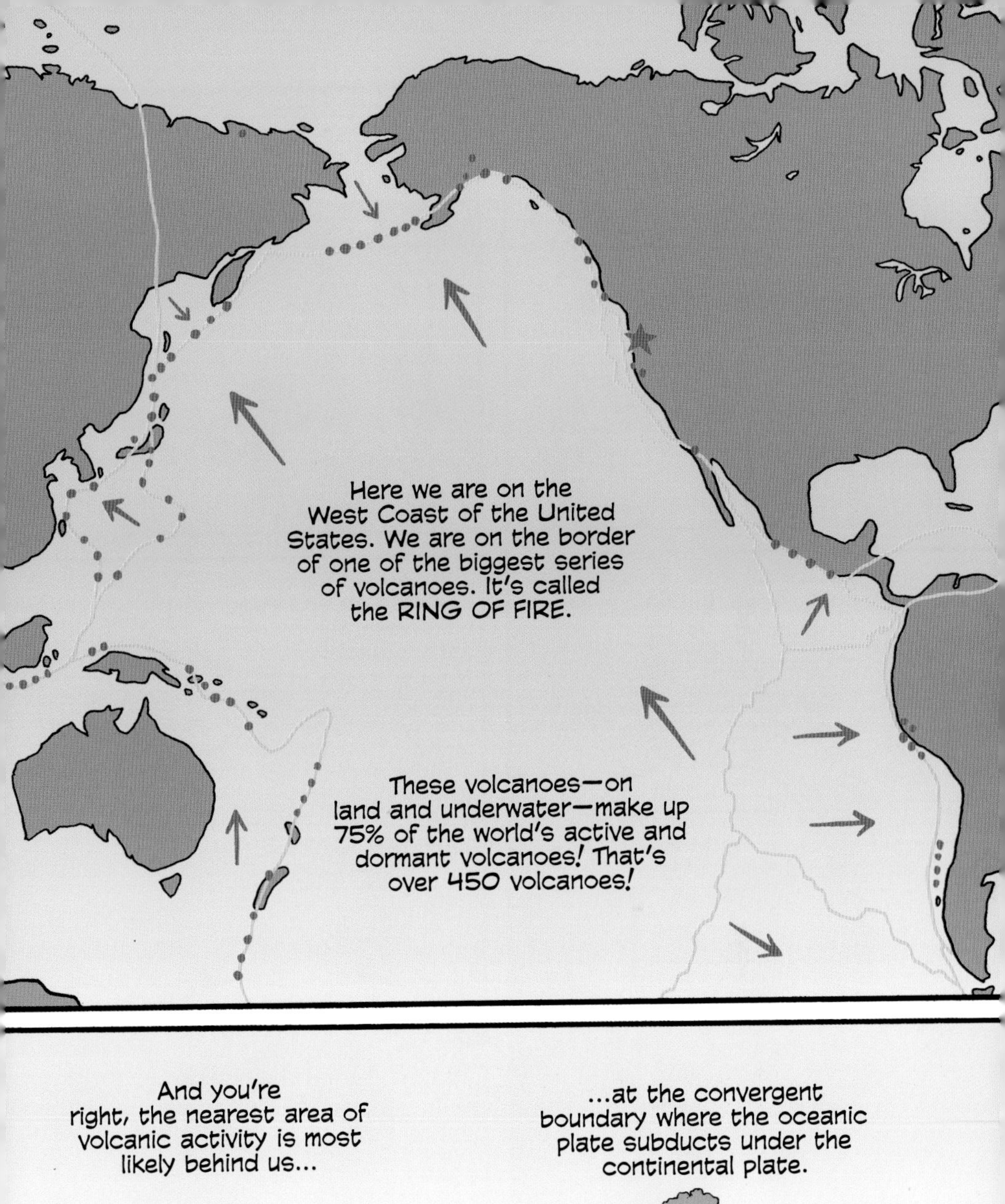
Here we are on the West Coast of the United States. We are on the border of one of the biggest series of volcanoes. It's called the RING OF FIRE.
These volcanoes—on land and underwater—make up 75% of the world's active and dormant volcanoes! That's over 450 volcanoes!

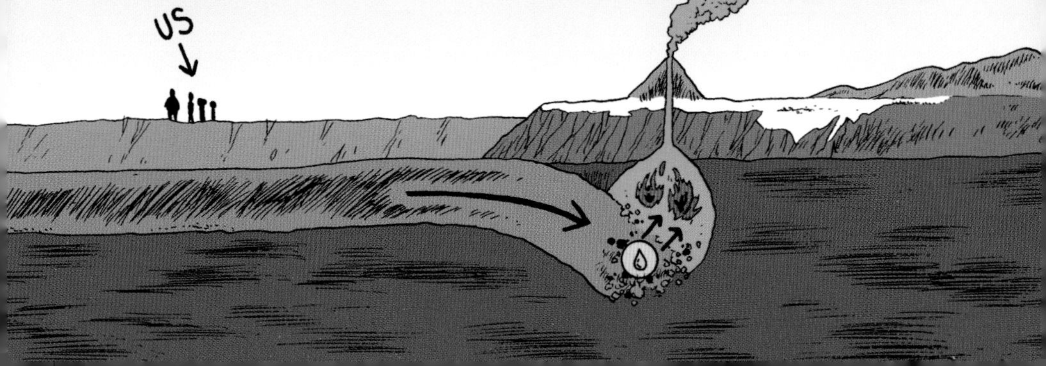
And you're right, the nearest area of volcanic activity is most likely behind us...
...at the convergent boundary where the oceanic plate subducts under the continental plate.
US

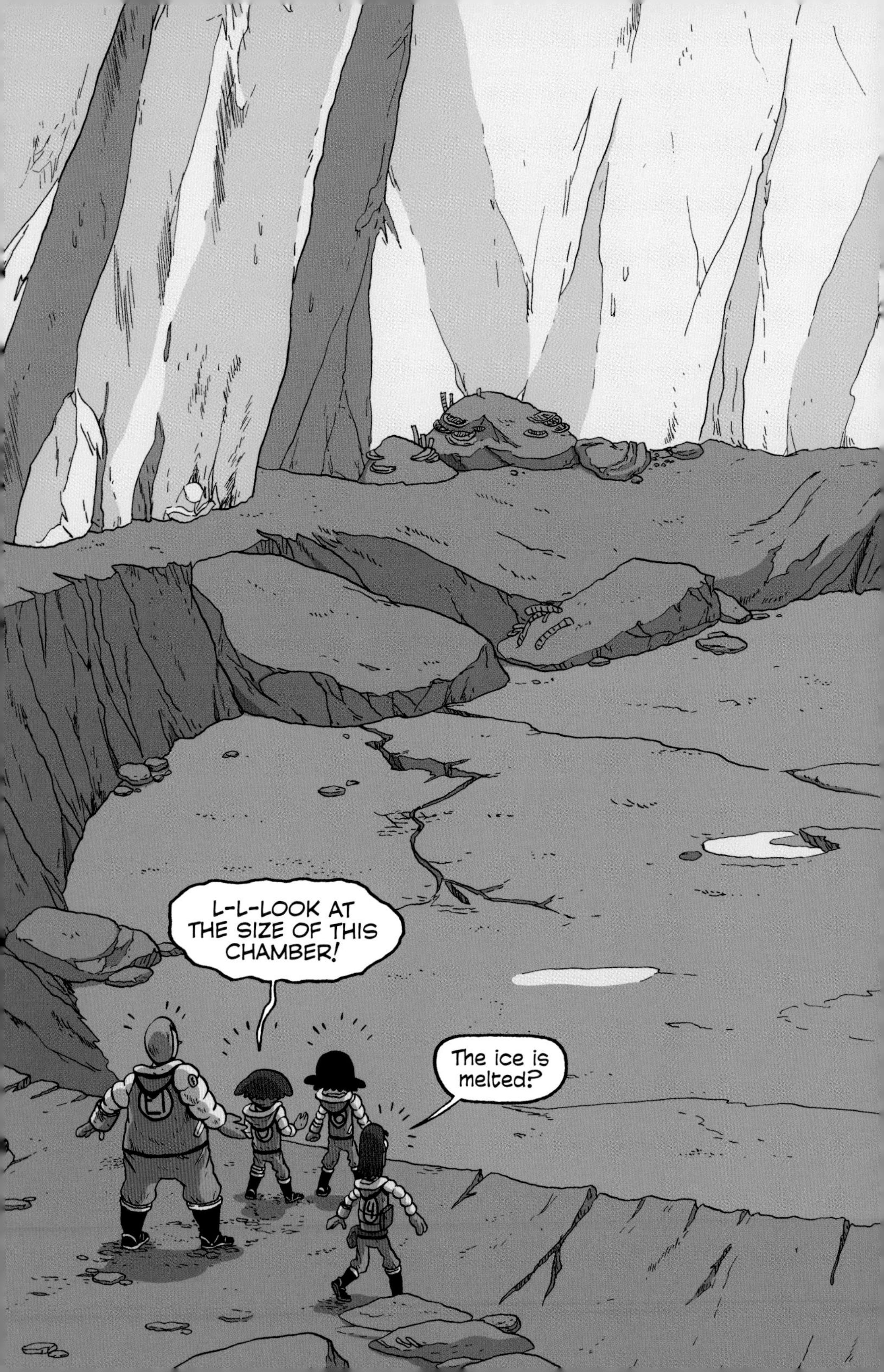
L-L-LOOK AT THE SIZE OF THIS CHAMBER!
The ice is melted?

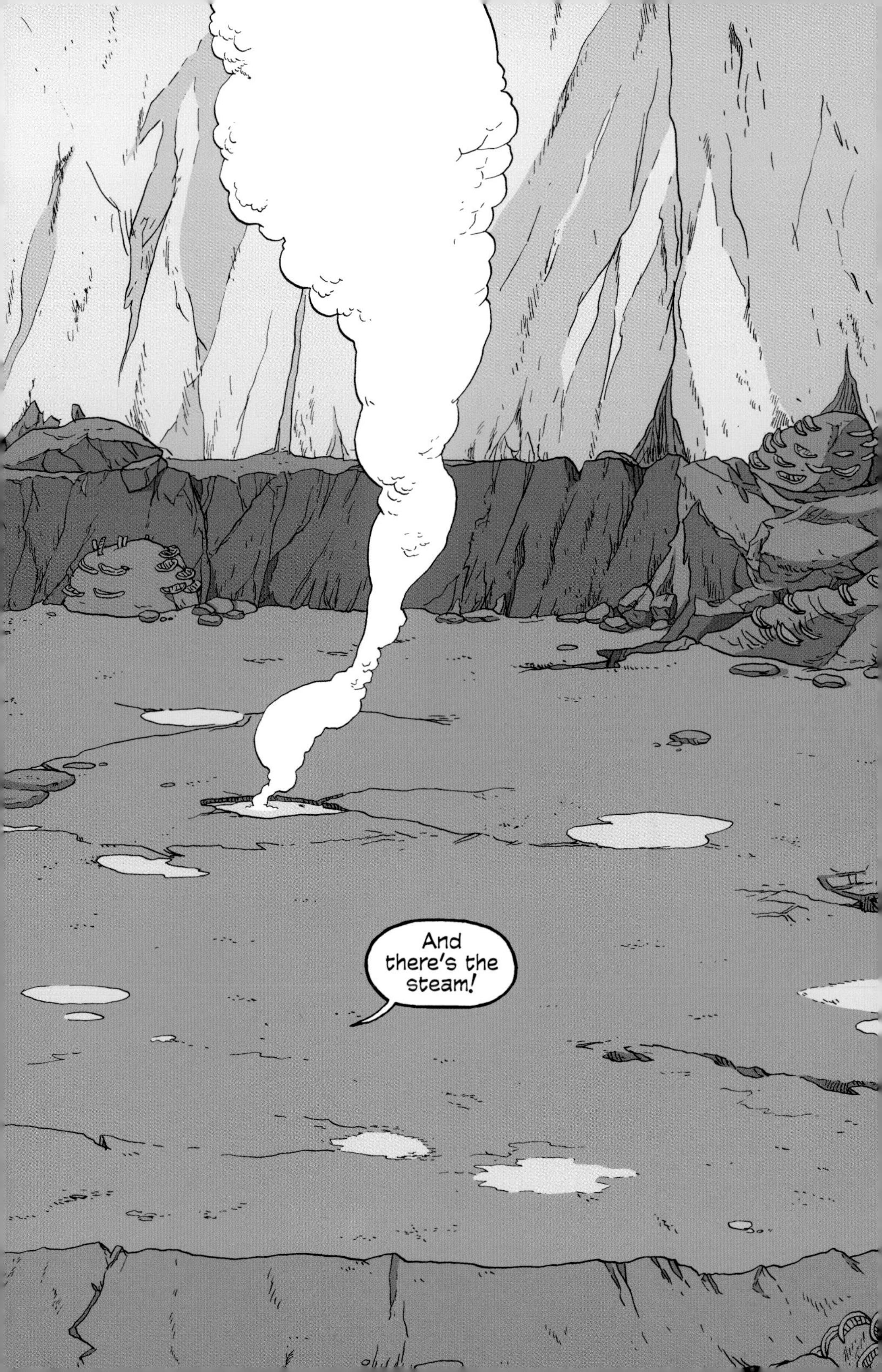
And there's the steam!

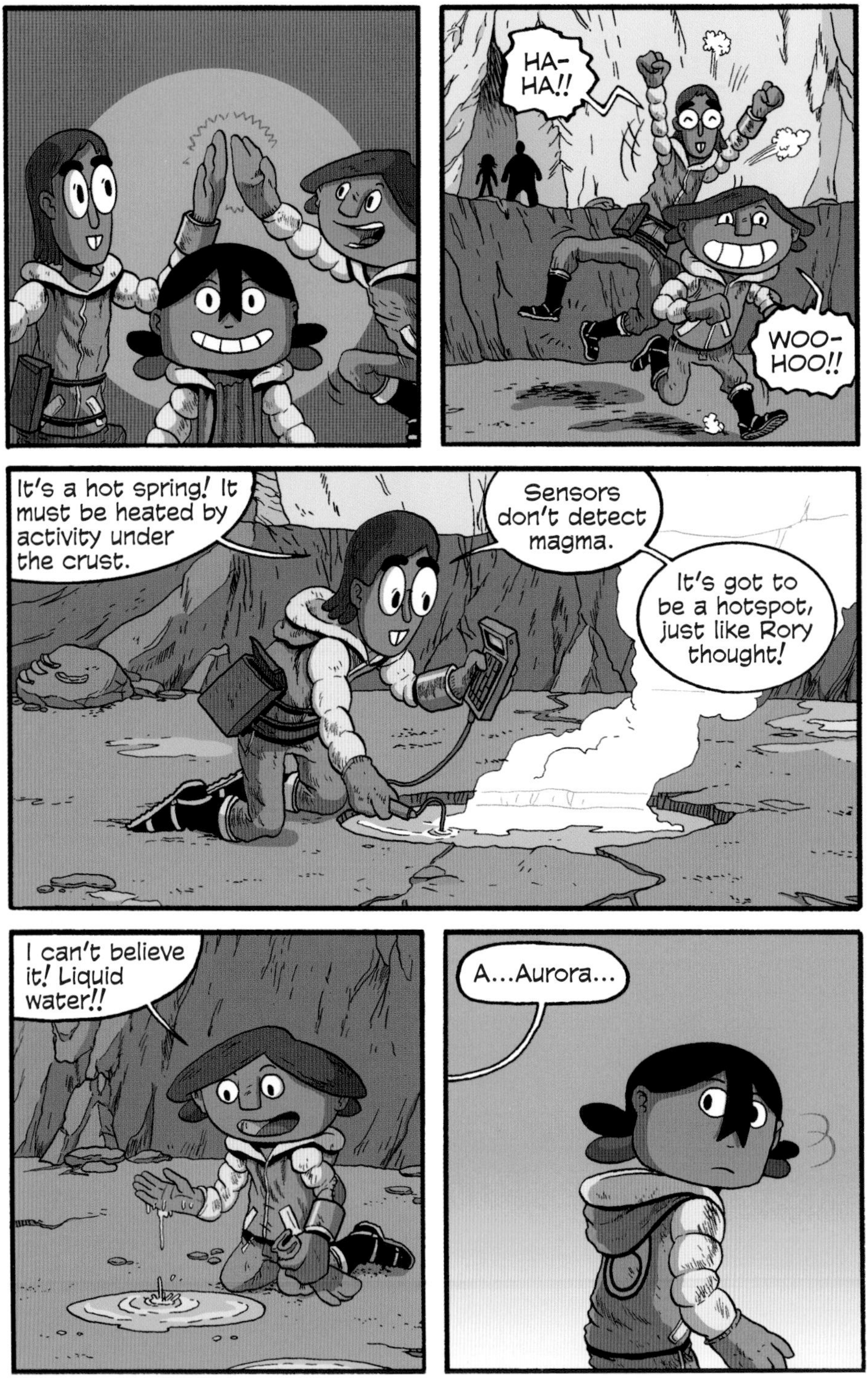
HA-HA!!
WOO-HOO!!
It's a hot spring! It must be heated by activity under the crust.
Sensors don't detect magma.
It's got to be a hotspot, just like Rory thought!
I can't believe it! Liquid water!!
A...Aurora...

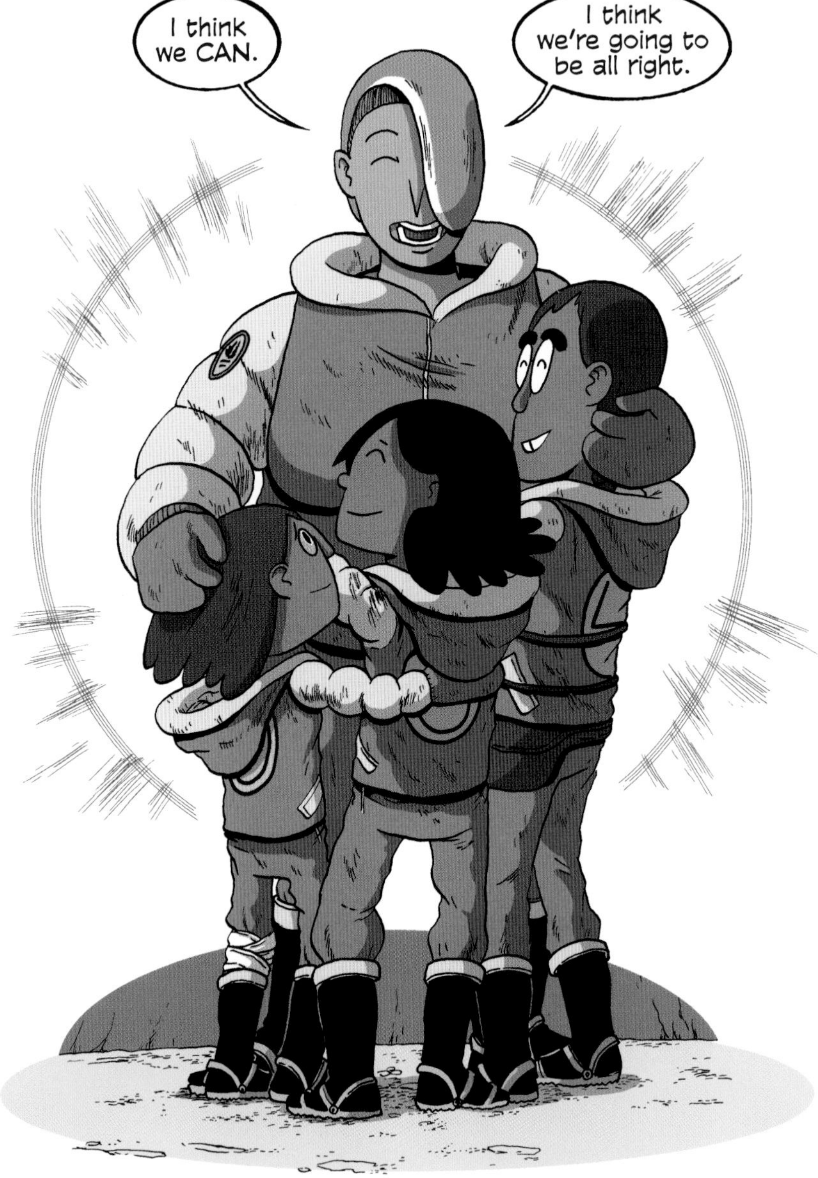
I think we CAN.
I think we're going to be all right.

VOCABULARY

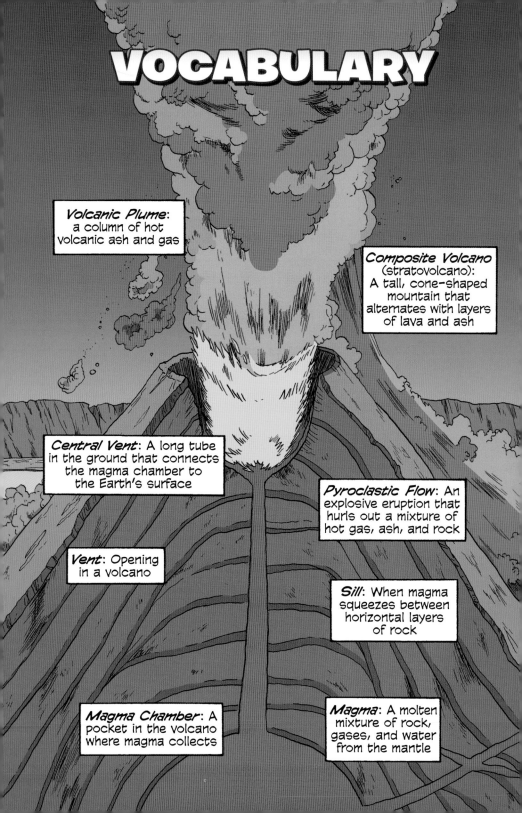

Volcanic Plume: a column of hot volcanic ash and gas

Composite Volcano (stratovolcano): A tall, cone-shaped mountain that alternates with layers of lava and ash

Central Vent: A long tube in the ground that connects the magma chamber to the Earth's surface

Pyroclastic Flow: An explosive eruption that hurls out a mixture of hot gas, ash, and rock

Vent: Opening in a volcano

Sill: When magma squeezes between horizontal layers of rock

Magma Chamber: A pocket in the volcano where magma collects

Magma: A molten mixture of rock, gases, and water from the mantle

Volcano: A weak spot in the crust where magma and gases erupts onto the surface

Ring of Fire: A major volcanic belt that covers parts of Asia, South and North America, and Australia

Island Arc: A string of islands

Hotspot: Where hot magma rises from the mantle/outer core border and through the crust. Unlike other types of volcanoes, these don't occur at plate boundaries.

Crater: Bowl-shaped area that may form around a volcano's central vent

Dormant: A volcano likely to awaken in the future, but currently inactive

Extinct: A volcano unlikely to ever erupt again

Caldera: The huge depression left by the collapse of a volcano with a depleted magma chamber

Cinder Cone: A steep volcano created by layers of ash, cinders, and rocks

Tectonic Plate: A huge portion of the Earth's crust that moves. There are two type of Tectonic Plates: heavier Oceanic Plates and lighter Continental Plates.

Viscosity: Liquid that is LESS viscous is thinner and runnier. Liquid that is MORE viscous is thicker.

Silica: A mixture of silicon and oxygen. More silica in magma makes it thicker and stickier.

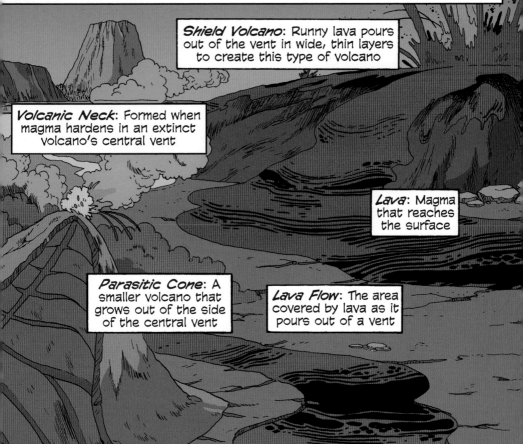

Shield Volcano: Runny lava pours out of the vent in wide, thin layers to create this type of volcano

Volcanic Neck: Formed when magma hardens in an extinct volcano's central vent

Lava: Magma that reaches the surface

Parasitic Cone: A smaller volcano that grows out of the side of the central vent

Lava Flow: The area covered by lava as it pours out of a vent

Interested in learning more about volcanoes?
Check out these cool books!

Gallant, Roy A. *Dance of the Continents*. New York: Benchmark Books, 2000.

Gallant, Roy A. *Plates: Restless Earth*. New York: Benchmark Books, 2002.

Gallant, Roy A. *Structure: Expoloring Earth's Interior*. New York: Benchmark Books, 2002.

Rosi, Mauro, Paolo Papale, Luca Lupi, Marco Stoppato. *Volcanoes*. New York: Firefly Books, 2003.

Stewart, Melissa. *Inside Volcanoes*. New York: Sterling Children's Books, 2011.

Thompson, Dick. *Volcano Cowboys: The Rocky Evolution of a Dangerous Science*. New York: St. Martin's Press, 2002.

Biography

Jon Chad is a cartoonist and illustrator living in Manchester Center, Vermont. He teaches bookmaking and design at the Center for Cartoon Studies and has done illustration work for the Professional & Amateur Pinball Association, *Highlights* magazine, and the FBI, among many others. He's also the author and artist of two other children's books, *Leo Geo and His Miraculous Journey Through the Center of the Earth* and *Leo Geo and the Cosmic Crisis*.

Sophie Goldstein is a 2013 graduate of the Center for Cartoon Studies. She won two Ignatz Awards for her graphic novel, *The Oven*, in 2015 and one for her mini-comic, *House of Women, Part I*, in 2014. Her work has appeared in various publications including *Best American Comics 2013*, *Fable Comics*, *The Pitchfork Review*, *Maple Key Comics*, *Sleep of Reason*, *Symbolia*, *Trip 8*, and *Irene 3*.

Thanks

Thank you to my friends and family. Thanks to Alec L, Alison W, Calista B, Casey G, Laura T, Luke H, Maris W, MK R, Sophie Y, and Stephen B for their support and guidance. Thanks to Kelly S for her help scanning and ruling out pages. Thank you to Gywn Hughes and Michael Cardiff for their amazing geology expertise, advice, and wisdom. Thanks to Sophie G for making this book come alive, and thanks to Tess Kahn for her love and friendship.